Al-Ghazali, Averroës and the Interpretation of the Qur'an

This book examines the contrasting interpretations of Islam and the Qur'an by Averroës and al-Ghazali, as a way of helping us untangle current impasses affecting each Abrahamic faith. This has traditionally been portrayed as a battle between philosophy and theology, but the book shows that Averroës was rather more religious and al-Ghazali more philosophical than they are usually portrayed.

The book traces the interaction between two Muslim thinkers, showing how each is convinced of the existence of a Book in which God is revealed to rational beings, to whom He has given commandments, as well as of the excellence of Islamic society. Yet they differ regarding the proper way to interpret the sacred Book. From this point of view, their discussion does not address the contrast between philosophy and religion, or that between reason and revelation that is so characteristic of the Middle Ages, but rather explores differences at the heart of philosophical discussion in our day: is there a level of discourse which will facilitate mutual comprehension among persons, allowing them to engage in debate?

This interpretation of sacred texts illustrates the ways religious practice can shape believers' readings of their sacred texts, and how philosophical interpretations can be modified by religious practice. Moreover, since this sort of inquiry characterizes each Abrahamic tradition, this study can be expected to enhance interfaith conversation and explore religious ways to enhance tolerance between other believers.

Avital Wohlman is Senior Lecturer in Philosophy at the Hebrew University of Jerusalem, exploring Scottus Eriugena, comparing Maimonides and Thomas Aquinas (1988, 1995), and here contrasts Ibn Rushd (Averroës) with al-Ghazali.

David Burrell is currently Professor of Ethics and Development at Uganda Martyrs University, and Hesburgh Professor Emeritus at University of Notre Dame, USA. He has compared Aquinas, Maimonides, and Avicenna; translated key works of al-Ghazali, and explored philosophical dimensions of human and divine freedom in the Abrahamic faiths.

Culture and civilization in the middle east

General Editor: Ian Richard Netton

Professor of Islamic Studies, University of Exeter

This series studies the Middle East through the twin foci of its diverse cultures and civilisations. Comprising original monographs as well as scholarly surveys, it covers topics in the fields of Middle Eastern literature, archaeology, law, history, philosophy, science, folklore, art, architecture and language. While there is a plurality of views, the series presents serious scholarship in a lucid and stimulating fashion.

Previously published by Curzon

The Origins of Islamic Law
The Qur'an, the Muwatta' and
Madinan Amal
Yasin Dutton

A Jewish Archive from Old Cairo
The history of Cambridge
University's Genizah collection
Stefan Reif

The Formative Period of Twelver Shi'ism
Hadith as discourse between
Qum and Baghdad
Andrew J. Newman

Qur'an Translation
Discourse, texture and exegesis
Hussein Abdul-Raof

Christians in Al-Andalus 711–1000
Ann Rosemary Christys

Folklore and Folklife in the United Arab Emirates
Sayyid Hamid Hurriez

The Formation of Hanbalism
Piety into power
Nimrod Hurvitz

Arabic Literature
An overview
Pierre Cachia

Structure and Meaning in Medieval Arabic and Persian Lyric Poetry
Orient pearls
Julie Scott Meisami

Muslims and Christians in Norman Sicily
Arabic-speakers and the end of Islam
Alexander Metcalfe

Modern Arab Historiography
Historical discourse and the
nation-state
Youssef Choueiri

**The Philosophical Poetics of
Alfarabi,
Avicenna and Averroes**
The Aristotelian reception
Salim Kemal

Published By Routledge

Al-Ghazali, Averroës and the Interpretation of the Qur'an

Common sense and philosophy in Islam

Avital Wohlman
Translated by David Burrell

Routledge
Taylor & Francis Group

LONDON AND NEW YORK

First published in French in 2008 as "Contrepoint entre
le sens commun et la philosophie en Islam Ghazali et Averroès"
by Editions du Cerf, Paris

First published in English in 2010
by Routledge
2 Park Square, Milton Park, Abingdon, Oxon OX14 4RN

Simultaneously published in the USA and Canada
by Routledge
270 Madison Ave, New York, NY 10016

Routledge is an imprint of the Taylor & Francis Group, an informa business

© 2010 Avital Wohlman

Typeset in Times New Roman by Swales & Willis Ltd, Exeter, Devon
Printed and bound in Great Britain by the MPG Books Group, UK

British Library Cataloguing in Publication Data
A catalogue record for this book is available from the British Library

Library of Congress Cataloging in Publication Data
Wohlman, Avital.
[Contrepoint entre le sens commun et la philosophie en Islam. English]
Al-Ghazali, Averroës and the interpretation of the Qur'an : common
sense and philosophy in Islam /Avital Wohlman, edited by David Burrell.
   p. cm.—(Culture and civilization in the Middle East; 19)
   Includes bibliographical references and index.
   1. Ghazzali, 1058–1111. 2. Averroës, 1126–98. 3. Philosophy, Islamic.
   4. Koran—Criticism, interpretation, etc.—History.
   I. Burrell, David. II. Title.
   B753.G34W5713 2010
   181'.07 – dc22
   2009021771

ISBN10: 0–415–55720–8 (hbk)
ISBN10: 0–203–86511–1 (ebk)

ISBN13: 978–0–415–55720–7 (hbk)
ISBN13: 978–0–203–86511–8 (ebk)

In memoriam of my distinguished master, Marcel-Jacques Dubois, O.P. (1920–2007) whose friendship accompanied me for more than thirty years and to the family of Yussuf Ibrahim Halil Aliane, who welcomed us into their midst in Beit Safafa

Contents

Translator's preface

David Burrell

While a seasoned student of ancient and medieval philosophy, Avital Wohlman has quite recently come to appreciate the Islamic dimensions of this field, and does so here in the manner characteristic of her work: to join issues directly and trenchantly. Moved by Sherman Jackson's translation of Ghazali's *Decisive criterion* (*On the Boundaries of Theological tolerance in Islam*, Sherman A. Jackson, [Karachi: Oxford University Press, 2002]), she wanted to grasp the import of the conflict this work had inspired in Averroës, so has delineated the sharp edges of that controversy. My offer to translate from her preferred language of composition, French, was motivated by respect for her philosophical acumen, as well as my need to grasp Averroës' thought better. Trying her best not to take sides, the author focuses on their profound disagreement regarding Qur'an interpretation, and in so doing, serves contemporary philosophical theologians by exploring issues which remain neuralgic. Averroës insists that any act of interpreting be philosophically informed, while Ghazali (in this work) would prefer intertextuality at best.

A concluding allusion to Josef Ratzinger's Regensburg address (2006) indicates the intended scope of her treatment. Averroës' debate with Ghazali is hardly limited to Islam, but envisages any revelational tradition: how much need believers have recourse to tools of philosophical analysis to delineate the coherence peculiar to their revealed texts? Speaking as Pope Benedict XVI (yet addressing Regensburg colleagues who had known him as Josef Ratzinger), his address noted how Christian tradition has been marked from the outset by a working dependence on philosophical strategies, notably to clarify the central doctrine of their faith in Jesus as the Word of God made human. In that sense, reason has ever been ingredient in appropriating Christian faith. Yet he stumbled in claiming that this was not the case in Islam. That uninstructed assertion, exacerbated by a misleading example, made pundits miss the focus of his discourse. It is that focus to which this work returns us, to highlight the myriad difficulties endemic to any public discussion of such matters, especially by one whose office represents a believing community. (In the wake of Regensburg, however, the generous response of Muslim intellectuals has in fact fomented a rich reprise of mutual inquiry among Christians and Muslims.)

For her part, Avital Wohlman delineates the diverse parameters of Islamic discussion of the role reason can play in interpreting Qur'anic texts, precisely by bringing the "exchange" between Ghazali and Averroës into sharp focus,. Indeed, showing how different are Ghazali's and Averroës' views on this matter forcibly reminds us how central such discussion has been in Islam. Yet she carries us a step further, to display the other side of the issue: how revelation can alter the use we make of philosophical strategies, and even transform those strategies themselves. In short, relations between reason and revelation can be mutually illuminating; and by expounding that dimension of Averroës' thought, this work effectively challenges a longstanding portrait of Averroës as a "rationalist." For whatever that clichéd term might mean, it bespeaks a mindset inclined to deny any intellectual relevance of faith to reason. Yet the Averroës we find addressing Ghazali, to insist that reason is indispensable in interpreting sacred texts, goes on invoke revelation to redress a longstanding lacuna in Aristotle's rational explication of the universe. That lacuna respects the source of the organization which makes the universe a unitary object of consideration: one world. Aristotle's everlasting species display an ordered finality proper to each, yet his touted "source of motion" falls short of explaining the order of the whole. Averroës introduces the "Artisan" to do just that, with palpable overtones of "creator." So the Qur'an has more to do with Averroës' metaphysics than many western commentators have presumed, precisely by offering a crucial emendation of Aristotle's metaphysics, in a way which completes it rather than undermines it. Such is her thesis, textually documented and carefully argued.

I have presumed to outline the thesis of this work, as its translator, since the challenge, in executing what should have been a relatively easy task (from French to English, whereas my other translations have been from Arabic to English), was exacerbated by the dense clarity of the author's philosophical exposition. Therein lies the merit of the fresh portrait of Averroës she offers: its very clarity allows it to be appreciated and challenged on its own merits. My own work on Ghazali convinces me that there are richer dimensions to him than this exchange displays, yet her unstinting focus on this specific exchange paradigmatically illustrates the way reason and revelation can be brought to interact, so as to enrich human understanding of these intractable issues. Indeed, we discussed these issues and the two Islamic thinkers thoroughly while she was composing the work itself in Beit Safafa, but a brief walk from my abode in the Tantur Ecumenical Institute in Jerusalem, all under the perspicacious eye and receptive ear of our mutual mentor, Marcel Dubois. As with countless scholars over the years, the personal and intellectual environment of Tantur made this work possible, through its rector, Fr. Michael McGarry, and its vice-rector, Sr. Bridget Tighe, who together create a home for students and scholars of all ages and nationalities, in a thirty-five acre oasis at a checkpoint, so that the realities of the Holy Land are never far away. In redacting the translation, we were both assisted incalculably by Marquette University graduate student, Ahmad Fuad Rahmat, who assiduously traced English equivalents for French translations employed by the author, and will earn special gratitude from readers for amplifying notes and bibliography to include relevant English texts for further reference. Indeed, our triadic relationship has made this work what it is.

Introduction

This book is devoted to the study of the "decrees" of al-Ghazali and of Averroës regarding the question which is found at the heart of Islamic existence, which may well be defined as being the "religion of the book" *par excellence*. In his *Decisive Treatise Distinguishing between Islam and the Hypocrites* (1045–6), Ghazali explains how, by pretending to know what eludes believers endowed with common sense alone, philosophers do not consider the Qur'an as revealed Word, and by thus failing to engage with its interpreters, by their very existence they threaten to destroy the identity of the Muslim community. In his *Book on the Decisive Criterion Whereby One Can Establish the Existing Connection between Revelation and Philosophy* (1179–80), which purports to be a response to al-Ghazali, Averroës sets out to show how philosophy alone can fully appreciate revealed truth, so it alone can guide one in interpreting the Qur'an in such a way as to preserve the absolute coherence of the "inimitable book."

This controversy is replete with consequences, but what particularly struck me about it is the way it is rooted in a discussion between two Muslim thinkers, each convinced both of the existence of a Book in which God is revealed to rational beings to whom He has given commandments, as well as of the excellence of Islamic society. Yet they differ regarding the criterion of interpreting the sacred Book.

From this point of view, the discussion between Averroës and Ghazali ought not to be considered to be one between philosophy and religion, or between reason and revelation, so characteristic of the Middle Ages, but rather like those which are at the heart of philosophical discussion in our day: is there a basic level of discourse which will permit mutual comprehension among persons, so that it may be presupposed by the very fact of debate? Like David Hume in the eighteenth century, and like many today, Ghazali is convinced that a level of discourse is available which authorizes rational inquiry and meaningful discussion outside any philosophy, by the light of common human experience in a manner unique to us as human beings. Averroës, on the other hand, is convinced that philosophy alone is able to resolve meaningful debates, so in its absence there will be nothing but diverse opinions and multiple experiences. Moreover, this is especially the case when it comes to the Word of God in the Qur'an: without philosophy, there can be no way of knowing its proper meaning. In this way, Averroës adopts the position of Aristotle, yet in the process refashions key concepts of Greek philosophy in the light of "revealed truth," thereby underscoring the rapport of revelation to philosophical activity. Similar to David Hume, Ghazali would rather limit reason to a critical capacity, as providing a necessary tool for realizing one's goal so long as those who use it respect its inherent limitations.

The vision of the world which David Hume presents in his *Treatise on Human Nature* (1748) resembles that presented by al-Ghazali in his *Incoherence of the Philosophers* (1094). Well before Hume, Ghazali did not want to neglect rational thought but rather to make room for common sense, by making it clear that there can be no domain reserved to philosophers. Both presume that human beings are susceptible of multiple impressions and habits acquired as a result of them. According to Ghazali and Hume, philosophers are imprisoned by their pretension that they alone are in possession of a unique mode of knowing, certain as the exact sciences and replete with consequences regarding existence itself. Yet in the face of this presumption and vainglory, their discussions only reflect verbal sparring. Yet contrary to Hume, who thought this to be the case universally, Ghazali gives central place to certitude concerning the existence of God, the sole agent, whose will constitutes the origin of all experience as well as determining the worth of all actions carried out by human beings in accomplishing His commandments, in fear and hope of His judgment.

In this way, the disagreement between Ghazali and Averroës regarding the criterion of interpretation of the Qur'an is coupled with the goal of revelation. Ghazali takes the goal to be deepening people's fear and hope regarding the last judgment, while Averroës takes it to be to encourage rational reflection on beings so as to expose better the beauty and marvelous coherence of the world as testimony to the perfection of the artisan whose very thought is creative. Ghazali is convinced that the literal sense of the Word of God is clear for the believer, especially in those passages which concern articles of faith; whereas Averroës, on the contrary, is intimately persuaded that only philosophers can identify the Qur'an's literal sense. For it is a unique Book whose miraculous veridical coherence will escape anyone bereft of the proper criterion of interpretation, which stems from logico-philosophical reflection on beings.

Nevertheless, the more Averroës highlights philosophical acumen as interpreter of the Qur'an, the more he feeds Ghazali's suspicion that philosophers are hypocrites, since they are not receptive of the truth of revelation but rather tout their power to assess it by the light of philosophical reflection. Indeed, according to Averroës, those who are not philosophers, like Ghazali, can hardly appreciate the profound affinity between revelation and philosophical activity, so will invariably fail to judge its proper valence. For his part, Averroës has treated this affinity in his works for philosophers, which for that very reason ought not be placed in the hands of those who are not philosophers.

Now both Ghazali and Averroës are agreed on this point: that public debate on the subject of faith and Qur'an interpretation can be the root of serious harm to the identity of believers and the cohesion of Islamic society, though this agreement will entail acutely disparate trajectories. For Ghazali, such debate is dangerous because it accentuates differences to the neglect of what is essential: the decisive equality among human beings as Muslims, who can only be distinguished by varying degrees of right intentions as well as the depth of hope which guides their journey towards the next world. Whereas for Averroës, public debate regarding the law and interpretation of the Qur'an will be corrupting because it is freighted with a double danger: trivialization of the Qur'an and obscuring the miraculous power of the inimitable Book, which is to convince all readers, even in the face of a categorical disparity in the degree of their respective modes of knowing.

The only way to resolve such impetuous debate, in the eyes of both Ghazali and Averroës, would be to place them under the severe and exigent control of a vigorous and intelligent authority. Ghazali hopes that such authority would respect the counsel of spiritual guides like himself, while Averroës hopes they would follow the counsel of philosophers. The gulf which separates us today from both Ghazali and Averroës can be displayed by the fact that neither of them envisaged the possibility that imposing silence on religious issues and debates over faith could lead to the secularization of society in such a way that the focus of worldly interest would henceforth be monopolized by utility and pleasure.

We can only comprehend the good to which Ghazali and Averroës aspired by removing debates concerning faith from public space in the light of the vitality of Muslim faith and the cohesion of Islamic society as they were then flourishing. Both spiritual master and philosopher relied upon the stability of Muslim life in a society all of whose members accepted the commandments of the Word of God in the Qur'an. In fact, this perfectly rooted and palpable stability explains why Averroës could accentuate radical differences among believers without disturbing their common practice. That same faith allowed Ghazali to call everyone to examine their consciences, the better to appreciate the gulf separating them from God considered in His ninety-nine perfections, yet remain keenly interested in imitating Him by deepening their fear and hope.

This fact will also help us understand the way the chapters are ordered to treat each theme of this discussion. The first chapter outlines aspects of their receptive biographies, where we find rooted their contrasting convictions regarding the role of reason: for Ghazali, a critical power and tool needed to realize the intentions of those who have taken its limits; for Averroës, the unique path to truth, an arena reserved to a select group beyond barriers of time or of language. There I shall also reflect on certain tendencies prevailing among commentaries on their two "decrees," to bring to light my debt to them as well as certain lacunae which I hope to supplant.

In the second chapter, taking account of the vicissitudes which appear to have shaped the life of Ghazali, with their possible import for the *Decisive Criterion of Distinction*, I attempt to clarify the sole preoccupation which animated his work before and during his eleven years of pilgrimage. I take note of the fact that Ghazali writes in the name and for the same audience, in the *Incoherence of the Philosophers*, the *Enlivening of Religious Knowing*, and the *Just Balance*, while at the same time challenging that same audience. In this way I concur with those authors who attribute a single motivation to Ghazali – that of being spiritual guide for ordinary Muslims, thereby distancing myself from those who attribute to him philosophical positions, or an esoteric theological perspective.

The third chapter is devoted to my interpretation of the *Decisive Criterion of Distinction*, in the light of Ghazali's stance regarding the strict agreement between the literal sense of the Word of God in the Qur'an and the conception of existence proper to common sense. The merit of this interpretation is that it will help us to read the fivefold disposition which this thinker proposes for reading the Qur'an by reference to his own examples, thereby revealing the strict rapport between this disposition and the literal sense of retribution promised to Muslims in the afterlife. So philosophers and certain Sufis who put their confidence in their intellectual or spiritual superiority are unmasked as hypocrites.

The object of Chapter Four is Averroës' response, explaining how philosophical inquiry is an explicit commandment of the Qur'an, hence obligatory for all who are capable of it. He will also underscore that the Qur'an cannot be an authoritative word unless the criterion for reading it has been established. Finally, he judges Ghazali to be acutely misled in condemning philosophers, whom he considers to be actively diverting people from faith. So this chapter in effect delineates the connection between revelation and philosophy from a philosophical point of view.

In Chapter Five I set out to study the original position of Averroës regarding the connection between revelation and philosophy from the point of view of revelation, as the Andalusian intellectual lays it out in works directed to philosophers. By way of introducing my position, according to which Averroës is a Muslim philosopher and an original interpreter of Aristotle, I will offer a summary presentation of the contrary view prevailing among most commentators. Basing myself on a naturalist interpretation of certain questions left open by Aristotle, I prepare the way to better appreciate better the different position held by the Muslim commentator. By studying his *Substance of the Celestial Sphere* as well as the *Large Commentary on the Metaphysics*, I hope to be able to show how his certain faith in the existence of the Artisan coheres with realigning the major concepts of Aristotelian metaphysics: nature, being, and matter. In the new alignment shaped by the light of faith, philosophical questions like the goodness of the world and its order become theological issues.

Chapter Six depends on the third and fourth chapters, to complete them by examining the social consequences of the positions of Ghazali and Averroës regarding the supremacy of a spiritual guide over against a philosopher in a society torn by debates. From his conviction regarding the utter equality of all Muslims as believers, Ghazali must justify the superiority of a spiritual guide, while Averroës must account for the place reserved for reasonable people who are not themselves philosophers, vis-à-vis the Qur'an. He must also fulfill his function as judge without attenuating the obligation of silence which his philosophical knowledge imposes on him, reserved as it is for philosophers.

Finally, I shall return, by way of conclusion, to the principles of the philosophical and religious debate which originated this study. I will first consider the two ways by which Ghazali and Averroës have organized the shared elements of their faith into two disparate theological configurations. I shall also underline the evident difference between the two models of society which they espouse. For while Ghazali retains a place in the heterogeneous society which Averroës endorses, Averroës has none in the society which Ghazali proposes. Finally, I shall outline the solution offered by the two thinkers with a view to ending the conflicts which they feel threaten the identity of Muslim believers. The solution they offer will illuminate the profound difference separating a strictly religious society, which allows the counterpoint we have limned between common sense and philosophy, from an "open," pragmatic and generally atheist polity of the west in our time.

For it remains a fact that Ghazali and Averroës intended to found their respective roles as first among believers on the silence assured by distancing debate about Qur'anic interpretation from the public domain. Both spiritual master and philosopher were intimately convinced that such debates were deadly for the religious conviction of the majority of Muslims. As much as we may well predict that philosophers who take such a position have failed to assess the way that silence of a rarely contemplative crowd can turn to violence, we may also wonder how this fact could have escaped a spiritual master. And if this be the case, it is hardly debates concerning Qur'an interpretation which threaten the holy Book, but rather their absence, which risks obscuring revelation by ossifying its limpid message.

In conclusion, let me list the works of Ghazali and of Averroës which I have used, whose authenticity is assured; along with their translations which have been wonderfully useful.

Abu Hamid ibn Muhammad al-Ghazali

Tahafut al-Falasifa (*L'incohérence des philosophes*) (Beirut: Bouyges, 1927; Cairo: Dunya, 1947). *The Incoherence of the Philosophers,* trans. M. E. Marmura (Provo, UT: Brigham Young University Press, 2000).

Ihya' Ulum ad-Din (*La revivification des sciences de la religion*) (Cairo: Halabi, 1er vol., 1346; 2ème, 3ème et 4ème vol., 1352/1933) Analysis and index by G.-H. Bousquet (Paris: Librairie Max Besson, 1955).

English translation of Book 35: *Faith in Divine Unity and Trust in Divine Providence*, translated with an introduction and notes by D. B. Burrell, C.S.C. (Louisville, KY: Fons Vitae, 2001).

Al-Maqsad al-Asna fi asma Allah al-husna (Cairo, 1324). English translation: *Al-Ghazali on the Ninety-Nine Beautiful Names of God* translated with notes by D. B. Burrell and N. Daher (Cambridge: Islamic Texts Society, 1995 / Louisville, KY: Fons Vitae, 2000).

Al-Qistas al-mustaqim (*La Balance juste*) (Cairo, 1900, Beirut: Victor Chelhot, 1959). French translation by Victor Chelhot, in *Bulletin d'É-tudes Orientales* XV, 7–98.

Faysal al-Tafriqa Bayn al-Islam wa az-Zandaqa (*Le décret de la distinction entre l'islam et les hypocrites*), in Jamahir al-Ghawali (Cairo: 1934, 75–104). English translation: *On the Boundaries of Theological*

Tolerance in Islam, Sherman A. Jackson, [coll. *Studies in Islamic Philosophy*, S. Nomanul Haq]. (Karachi: Oxford University Press, 2002); French translation: *Le critère décisif de distinction entre l'islam et le manichéisme*. Présentation, traduction, étude sémiotique par Mustapha Hogga (Bordeaux: Bibliothèque universitaire, 1983).

Al-Munqidh min al-dalal (*Erreur et délivrance*), (Cairo: Qasim, 1952); (Beirut: UNESCO, 1959). English translations: W. M. Watt, *The Faith and Practice of Al-Ghazali* (London: G. Allen and Unwin, 1967); R. J. McCarthy, *Freedom and Fulfillment* (Boston: Twayne Publishers, 1980), re-issued as *Al-Ghazali's Deliverance from Error* (Louisville, KY: Fons Vitae, 2005); French translation: Farid Jabre, *Erreur et délivrance*, with introduction and notes (Beirut: Commission libanaise pour la traduction des chefs-d'œuvre, Beirut, 2ème éd., 1969).

Abu'l Walid Muhammad ibn Ahmed ibn Rushd, or Averroës

Bidaya al-Mujtahid wa nihayat el-Munqtasid (*Le commencement pour celui qui s'efforce et la fin pour celui qui se satisfait*) (Cairo: Halabi, 3ème éd., 1960).

G. F. Hourani (éd.), *Damima al-Ilm al-Ilahiy* (*Appendice à la science de la métaphysique*) (Leiden: E. J. Brill, 1959); English translation in G. F. Hourani, *Averroës on the Harmony of Religion and Philosophy* (London: Luzac & Co., 1976).

G. F. Hourani (éd.), *Fasl al-Maqal wa Taqrir Ma bayn al-Shariah wa l-Hikma min al-Ittisal* (*Le discours décisif du rapport entre religion et philosophie*) (Leiden: E. J. Brill, 1959); English translation by G. F. Hourani under the title: *Averroës on the Harmony of Religion and Philosophy* (London: Luzac & Co., 1976); *The Book of the Decisive Treatise Determining the Connection Between the Law and Wisdom with Epistle Dedicatory*, tr. Charles Butterworth [English/Arabic] (Provo, UT: Brigham Young University Press, 2001). French translation under the title *Le Livre du discours décisif*, introduction par Alain de Libera, trad. inédite, notes et dossier par Marc Geoffroy (Paris: Flammarion, 1996).

Al-Kashf an manahij al-Adillah (*Exposition des méthodes de la preuve*), *Al-Matbaat al-Rahmaniyyah* (Cairo, n.d.), partial English translation by G. F. Hourani (London: Luzac & Co., 1961).

Ibn Rushd's Metaphysics, a translation with introduction of *Ibn Rushd's Commentary on Aristotle's Metaphysics*, *Book Lamda* (XII), by Charles Genequand (Leiden: F. J. Brill, 1984).

Averroës' De Substantia Orbis, Critical edition of the Hebrew text with English translation and commentary by Arthur Hyman (Cambridge, MA and Jerusalem, 1986).

Averroës on Plato's Republic, translated with an introduction and notes by R. Lerner (Ithaca, NY and London: Cornell University Press, 1974).

Tahafut at-Tahafut (Incohérence de l'incohérence), Bibliotheca Arabica Scholasticorum, Arabic Series n 3, M. Bouyges (Beirut: Imprimerie catholique, 1930); English translation by Van den Bergh: *Averroës' Tahafut al-Tahafut (The incoherence of the incoherence)* (London: Luzac, 1954).

Chapter 1

Journeys of Ghazali and Averroës to their diverse conceptions of the role of reason

Preamble

The different conceptions of Ghazali and Averroës regarding what is required of believers stem from different circumstances in their respective lives. For Ghazali, faith is an intention of the heart which is rooted in Muslim life to inspire people's choices and realize them in their daily lives by having recourse to reason. For Averroës, faith is what awakens a pressing desire, in those capable of it, to enter into the lucid plenitude of God's revelation in the Qur'an.

The initial section of this chapter will be devoted to Ghazali's journey. The son of a simple pious Muslim, he had fulfilled his father's hopes by becoming director of the greatest academy in Baghdad, capital of the Abbassid empire, only to precipitously renounce his post for eleven years of pilgrimage. As he himself will write, this decision had been inspired by Sufi teaching received from infancy. At the end of this prolonged retreat he returned to Baghdad, and then to his birthplace of Tûs in Iran. Yet these peregrinations should not distract us from the unique intention animating them.

I shall devote the second part of this chapter to the studious and sedentary life of Averroës, utterly different, as it turned out, from the mobile existence of Ghazali. Son of a family of high court judges already established for three generations in Cordoba, the Andalusian philosopher had a settled place in the society of his time, well suited to carrying out philosophical inquiry. This explain why he was so grateful to God for the grace of living under the good government of the Almohad dynasty in Muslim Spain.

A third part will focus on the divergent approaches of commentators on the "decrees" of Ghazali and Averroës, as a way of directing the renewed interest I hope to inspire in their work.

Part one – Abu Hamid ibn Muhammad al-Ghazali

Abu Hamid ibn Muhammad al-Ghazali was born in 1058 in Tûs, in the province of Khorassan in northeast Iran, in the heart of a rigorously hier-archical society, at a time when theologians and Sunni jurisprudents held sway over the Muslim world. In the second half of the eleventh century, the Abbassid empire with its capital in Baghdad, endured thanks to a del-icate balance among the caliph, the Seljuk sultans, army generals, and ministers (who were Persian functionaries). At the service of a Sunni con-ception of power, the military was charged with protecting and fortifying the Abbassid empire, extending from Afghanistan to the Mediterranean, in its ongoing battle with the Fatimids, who after conquering north Africa, had established a Shi'ite polity, with Cairo as their capital. Opposition between Sunni and Shi'ite conception of power is rooted in the twofold mission of Muhammad, religious and socio-political, at the heart of a community called to become Muslim.

At the death of the Prophet of Islam, this opposition solidified into two views concerning his successor. Did Muhammad designate his successor in giving any hint concerning the way of devolving power? This question, left to posterity, would engender a dual debate. One concerns the func-tions of the caliph or imam, held jointly by the Prophet during his life: should they remain in the hands of one person? The other concerns the principle involved in designating a successor: should it be electoral or transcendent? Shi'ite teaching holds that the community must submit to a divine decree mediated by the family of Muhammad, itself endowed with exceptional qualities; whereas in the Sunni conception, the mode of elec-tion may vary: a choice carried out by the entire community or by some of its members. The ideological conflict between these two conceptions led to a war of succession after the period of the four initial caliphs, called "rightly guided," who directed the umma (the community of Muslim believers) one after another, according to various modes of investiture: Abu Bakr (632–34), Omar (634–44), Othman (644–56), and Ali (656–61). The assassination of Othman, in 656, crystallized these antago-nisms. On one side were the partisans of Ali, cousin and descendent of Muhammad, to whom he had married his daughter Fatima: the inhabitants of Medina (Yathrib, become Medina al-Nabi – the city of the Prophet), who were devoted to that quality of religious understanding and scrupu-lous observance of the Qur'an associated with Ali. On the other were cer-tain Meccan families associated with Othman, whom the Shi'ites had considered a usurper.[1] One must realize that the actions of theologians and

of Sunni jurisprudents was of immense value to an Abbassid empire con-
fronted with the criticism of the Fatimids. Their activity was also of primary importance to the Seljuk military leadership, of Turkish origin and
newly converted to Islam, whose power rested on religious consent.
Finally, Sunni jurisprudents and theologians had the mission of giving
support to the Abbassid empire by presenting it as the faithful representative of the best of Persian culture.[2]

From leaders to simple believers, all strata of society were suffused
with a deep veneration of learned religious persons, so Ghazali's father
had raised his two sons to be like them. The son acquiesced to the desires
of his father, giving himself totally to the study of the law and Islamic theology, both of which remain central preoccupations during all four recognized phases of his life.[3] At his death, the father willed his estate to a Sufi
master for the education of his children. The Abbasid-Seljuk aristocracy
never regarded Sufi spirituality as a threat to their authority; they rather
viewed it as a crucial supporting pillar to consolidate and preserve the
social order, considering the central place which examination of conscience and struggle against passions held in the life of Sufis on their journey to the afterlife according to Qur'anic commandments.

Ghazali considered purification of intention and fidelity to God's commands to be the foundation of the life of any believer who places their confidence [tawakkul] in the one unique God [tawhid]. He had learned
jurisprudence [fiqh] in his hometown before leaving for Nishapur, where
he undertook studies with the most prestigious masters of the time, especially the Ash'ari imam Abdul Maali el-Juwayni, until the master's death
in 1085. On the basis of this intellectual formation, Ghazali adhered to the
Shafi' school of law as well as the Asha'rite theological school, which
teaches an intimate link between the one God and God's spiritual attributes – those perfections designated by "the ninety-nine beautiful names."
He never renounced this doctrine,[4] despite his growing insistence that one
renounce the pleasures of dialectic and of critical reason.[5]

So Ghazali acquired the reputation of a young scholar with the special
talent of summarizing the thought of other intellectuals with clarity and
precision. His Arabic rendition of the work of the Persian work of
Avicenna [Danesh Nameh], as the Intentions of the Philosophers
[Maqasid al-falasifa], amply manifests this talent. Avicenna had delineated the heart of his metaphysics, showing the affinity between
Hellenistic philosophy and Muslim faith.[6] Ghazali's synthesis preceded
and supported his critical work, the Incoherence of the Philosophers
(1091), composed in the light of what he took to be essential in the
Intentions of the Philosophers: the vanity of those who had unlimited con-

fidence in the power of reason to articulate the very foundation of existence.

With this critical stance, Ghazali underwrote the hope of Abbassid-Seljuk political leaders to unify the religious foundation of their empire, considering him specially equipped to contribute to consolidating a cultural and religious ethos. So in 1091, only thirty-four years old, he was chosen to direct the distinguished academy of Baghdad, the Nizamiyya. For a subtle and lasting balance obtained among the Sunni caliph, al-Mustazahir, his army commander (1072–92), Malik Shah I, and his vizier, Nizam al-Mulk, a brilliant statesman whose name will grace the institution charged with teaching various strategies for interpreting the Qur'an, whose masters and students were destined to animate the political structures of the Abbassid empire.[7]

Ghazali carried out his commission with distinction from 1091 to 1095, displaying to numerous auditors his capacity to unite younger intellectuals by helping them attend to essentials shared by all believers. Then suddenly in 1095 he resigned from the academy, replaced himself with his brother and disappeared from public view for eleven years, during which he traveled to Syria and Palestine, making pilgrimages to Mecca and Medina. Prayer took first place in this period of exile, when he revised the forty books of his *Revivication of Religious Learning* [*Ihya' ulum ad-din*], whose widespread dissemination reinforced his activity as spiritual guide. Many hypotheses have attempted to explain this abrupt change of venue: fear of the Ismailis, an especially violent Shi'ite faction whose members had assassinated his patron, Nizam al-Mulk, in 1092; misguided political calculations which might have deterred Ghazali from supporting the Seljuk sultan Barkiyaruk, whom he felt would not support him were he to assume power; and finally, that God himself had facilitated his deliverance from the distractions and sheer machinations which he had suffered up to that point, as he himself reports in his autobiographical account, *Error and Deliverance*, composed in 1106 when he returned to Nishapur after the death of Barkiyaruk (1105).[8] It was God who had helped save him from the distractions and evasions in which he had hitherto indulged.

We may now recognize Mustapha Hogga's suggestion to contextualize Ghazali's "confessions" in their socio-political setting to be utterly appropriate. For Ghazali had been deeply convinced that his activity at the heart of the Nizamiyya, as well as his contribution to consolidating the Sunni polity against Shi'ite encroachment had been religiously valuable. From this perspective, he hardly thought of himself as an ordinary subject of political powers, but rather as a co-worker active in realizing a Muslim society worthy of the name. His struggle against Shi'ism was rooted in a deep conviction that the Word of God in the Qur'an could never be restricted to an intellectual elite, just as power cannot simply belong to a class endowed with exceptional gifts. Indeed, this conviction that the Qur'an, which defines itself as written "in a clear Arabic," is accessible to all believers explains how disconcerting it would be for Ghazali to discover the social-political entanglements which had induced Barkiyaruk to found his power so successfully on relations with the Shi'ite *Batiniyya* – a movement which regarded the authentic meaning of the Qur'an to be obscured from everyone but the hidden Imam, whom they held to be infallible.

In the light of all that, how could he regard his own success in the *Nizamiyya* except as a serendipitous coincidence of his own quest for excellence being useful to Nizam al-Mulk in carrying out his own intentions? Yet he had to yield to the hopes of his father and his Sufi master rather than rely unconditionally on Abbassid-Seljuk power. So believing as he did in this profound conviction that the Qur'an must be accessible to all believers, he was inspired to mobilize his intellectual and critical powers to distance both students and professors at the *Nizamiiyya* from the vanity of philosophers in the name of their faith in the excellence of the Qur'an.[9]

At once the spokesman as well as spiritual guide of ordinary Muslims, the singular motive inspiring all Ghazali's writings before his departure from Baghdad and during his years of retreat will be the subject of our second chapter, while the third will be devoted to the "decree" redacted by Ghazali after he had returned to academic activity in a satellite of the *Nizamiyya* in Nishapur, at the invitation of Fakhr al-Mulk, the son of Nizam al-Mulk. This same motive will offer clear evidence as well on why he retired yet again in 1096, settling definitively in Tûs to devote himself to prayer and study in the company of a few students. It was there that he died in 1111.

Nor was Averroës unaware of this single-minded intention which motivated Ghazali's testy battle with the philosophers. According to the judge of Cordoba, commentator of Aristotle, this intention sufficed to identify the immense harm that pious and well-intentioned spiritual masters could cause once they were persuaded that everyone was well-equipped to comprehend the Word of God. He never questioned the faith which animated Ghazali, but still considered that, as a spiritual guide far from the practice of a philosophical inquiry whose very concepts outstripped him, he could not but mislead his auditors. For should some of them manage to raise questions which he could not answer, that very fact could awaken in them doubts prone to threaten the integrity of their faith.

Now to understand what led Averroës to develop his conception of the role of reason, we proceed to recount his itinerary.

Part two – Abu'l-Walid Muhammad ibn Rushd, Averroës

Abu'l-Walid Muhammad ibn Ahmed ibn Rushd [Averroës] opens his *Decisive Treatise* by underlining his two titles of judge and scholar.[10] He closes it by giving thanks to God for granting him the grace to live in the Almohad polity, and so bringing to light two signal attributes of power: the use of force and the empowerment of "that class of persons who are engaged on the path of rational inquiry and aspire to knowledge of the truth."[11]

It was indeed by force that the Almohads brought the cultured yet waning Almoravide polity to a close in 1147, just before Averroës was born in 1126. He was the grandson and son of a line of Maliki judges in Cordoba, a vital Andalusian cultural center where literary personages as well as Maliki judges (who traced their lineage to the tradition of Medina, the city of the Prophet) enjoyed the esteem of the emir Ali ibn Yussuf. Too weak to put an end to the internecine battles of heads of families thirsty for power, he was also incapable of stemming the reconquista of Christian armies threatening his polity from the outside. This subtle rapport among various forms of the love of letters, literary and jurisprudential, may well have formed the basis for Averroës' commentary on Plato's *Republic*, explaining how the absence of strong government is accompanied by a despotic hedonism.[12]

The "vanquishing power" of the Almohads would bring these ravages to an end, thereby permitting the extended career of Averroës to flourish, as well as fulfilling the desires extant among his grandfather and certain friends and masters under the Almoravides.[13] It is also worth emphasizing that despite the Maliki tradition to which grandfather, father and he himself belonged as judges, Averroës felt free to defend diverse juridical positions, even those opposed to his school, thereby imitating his elders. Even more, despite the dominance of Maliki judges under the Almoravides, Averroës' grandfather succeeded in liberating Ibn Bajja [Avempace] from prison, where he had been sentenced for having renounced the faith. Furthermore, as yet more evidence of Almoravid liberalism, Ghazali's *Revivication of Religious Learning*, in which he denigrates Maliki judges for their deviance as well as moral and religious aberrations, was able to be published in Cordoba.[14]

Yet it could also have been that this intellectual openness was accompanied by a certain lack of rigor which affected Makili jurisprudents. The

Maliki school rested on the conviction that since the Qur'an was not a book like others, it could not be interpreted outside a contextual reading proper to the Prophet himself. Hence their need to return to the tradition of Medina as the source of precedents which they made it a point of honor to follow. Nevertheless, in the face of multiple Medinan traditions, they had to confront debates regarding their proper identification and the order of their appearance. Yet in these debates they no longer followed the precedents of the Prophet and his companions, but rather their own masters, which explains why they attributed the following names to their adversaries: men of opinion [ra'y], imitators, and traditionalists.[15]

Nonetheless, it is clear that the existence of various Medinan traditions posed a real problem for the Maliki school, threatening its very foundation – a problem which had preoccupied Averroës' grandfather, the supreme judge and imam of the great mosque of Cordoba, who died the year his grandson was born. The title of his work, *Prefaces* [al-Muqaddamat] suggests its aim: to clarify the exigencies wrought by qualifications to the laws [al-mudawwana] governing legal sentences according to solid legal traditions, in an effort to offer an account of principal problematic questions.[16] Far from being yet another opinion [ra'y], he rather makes the revolutionary proposal that debates about different traditions should not try to cohere with precedents, but rather follow the light of their roots [usul], that is, Qur'anic verses themselves.

Averroës' grandfather clarifies this strategy at the outset of his book:

> only those aware of the obligations which the laws impose can hope to scrutinize divine law properly, and the only way to know these obligations would either be to know God, His essential attributes and His actions, or to follow the signs He gives in lieu of proofs. But only those endowed with reason are able to speculate and carry the proof to its term.[17]

Of the two ways which the author proposes to account for divine law, the first, which relies on intuition of the divine essence with its attributes, is closer to the Ash'arite conception, while that which scrutinizes Qur'anic verses is preferred by Averroës yet reserved to those endowed with what he calls "deep knowledge," as we shall see.[18] The first way will be rejected by Ibn Tûmart, founder of the Almohad line, who denied divine attributes in the name of absolute divine unicity.[19]

Ibn Tûmart had arrived in North Africa in 1118 as a preacher eliciting the revitalization of religion by returning to the roots of Muslim faith. He presented himself as the Mahdi, representing the infallibility of God on earth, forcefully criticizing Maliki judges who preferred subjective and fallible human opinion to the veridical and objective foundation of divine revelation. Moreover, according to Ibn Tûmart, anyone is able to comprehend the foundation of revelation, which is the absolute dependence of limited and mortal human beings on their creator.[20] He identifies this acute dependence of each human being on the creator as the second dimension of self-consciousness, which is common to all human beings in so far as they are conscious beings.

Two years after his death in 1130, Ibn Tûmart's charge passed to Abdu Mumin, a brilliant statesman and military leader. He destroyed the Almoravid polity in 1147, and was acknowledged and admired by the Muslim princes of Spain to the point of acquiring the title "Prince of believers" by the time Averroës reached the age of twenty-one. He had already completed at this time his studies in the three fields which would form the basis for his long and fertile career at the heart of Almohad power: law, medicine, and philosophy; first under the aegis and at the service of Abu Yacub Yussuf (1163–84) and then Abu Yussuf Yacub al-Mansur (1184–99).

Averroës had mastered Maliki jurisprudential skills with al-Hafiz Abu Muhammad ibn Rizq, with critical attention to traditions [*hadiths*]. He also studied with Ibn Bashkuwal, the student of his grandfather, so had been initiated in the work we have mentioned, *Prefaces* [*al-Muqaddamat*]. He carried out his medical studies with Abu Jafar ibn Harun al-Targali. A resident of Seville, acclaimed for his competence in treating eye disease, he was an exceptionally erudite man whose competence extended to jurisprudence and philosophy as well, notably the biological works of Aristotle. And even though Avempace has not been mentioned, we can presume that Averroës knew him, if only through his grandfather's intercession to free him from prison. We may suppose that this event helped to sensitize the young Averroës to the harm which those neither versed in speculation nor in proofs can cause to persons of "deep knowledge."[21] Ibn Tufayl [Abubacer, d. 1185], a philosopher and the personal physician of the caliph Abu Yacub Yussuf, and friend of Averroës, will insert this categorical difference between the "many" and the elite at very the heart of his philosophical novel, *Hayy ibn Yaqzan* [*A Philosophical Tale*].[22] It tells the story of an infant reared by a gazelle who reaches full discovery of the whole of natural truths, metaphysical and religious, in their coherence and congruence with divine revelation in the Qur'an. Not wishing to undertake the education of his peers, this young hero was constrained to flee a society replete with disorder stemming from the violent desires of the "many," to devote himself to a reclusive regime of study, which Avempace considered to be the only one compatible with philosophic life.

In 1169, Ibn Tufayl introduced his brilliant young friend, Averroës, to Abu Yacub Yussuf (d. 1184). Averroës had already completed an initial version of his juridical treatise, in which he defended a jurisprudence inspired by its roots (usul) in Qur'anic verses.[23] The caliph took an interest in him, encouraging him to continue his work, and especially his commentaries on Aristotle.[24]

Current commentators divide regarding their evaluation of the position of the Almohad caliph, depending on the stance they take regarding Almohad power. Some thinkers find this power to have been motivated by the desire to realize the vision of Ibn Tûmart, and would find evidence of the foundation of educational circles obligatory for all along the lines of the principle of the unicity of God.[25] Others rather subscribe to the eulogy of Averroës, crediting him with recognizing the worth of philosophical activity in Islam.[26] Those who doubt that the caliph had any real attraction to philosophy will see his interest in Averroës limited to soliciting him to use his capacities for a public role in the educational system.[27]

Yet the subject of the conversation among Averroës, the caliph, and Ibn Tufayl was indeed metaphysics, and notably the relation between everlasting heavenly movement and its dependence on the creator.[28] In describing this encounter, the historian, al-Marakushi, says that Averroës was not at ease, so in an effort to inspire confidence, the caliph laid out diverse opinions of Muslim scholars and philosophers on this subject.[29] I would concur with Marc Geoffroy, who finds the caliph's interest to be sincere, so that Averroës was not fooled when he recognized the caliph as a leader who clearly perceived the properly religious value of philosophical inquiry, and so would count as one of those to whom the Decisive criterion would be directed.[30]

In 1169–70, Averroës was named judge [qadi] of Seville, a clear indication that his philosophical activity raised no suspicion whatsoever regarding his religious orthodoxy. Between 1170 and 1178 he worked on interpreting the Physics, the Rhetoric, and the Metaphysics of Aristotle, as well as on his own original work, On the substance of the celestial sphere [de substantia orbis], devoting the next two years to responding to al-Ghazali's attacks on the philosophers. By 1179, in the Decisive criterion, he undertook to give an account of the role of philosophical inquiry and its absolute necessity for interpreting the "inimitable book." The following year found him occupied in responding to the Incoherence of the philosophers, in an effort to address the same public as Ghazali, that is, ordinary believers, to alert them that the spiritual master had proposed no valid reason to justify rejecting (as he had) the vision transmitted by Aristotle of a world perfectly intelligible and coherent.

In 1182 Averroës succeeded Ibn Tufayl as personal physician of the caliph, and was named chief judge [*qadi*] of Cordoba. After Abu Yussuf Yacub (al-Mansur) came to power, Averroës moved to Marrakesh, where he enjoyed the caliph's favor, but his long and fruitful life of study came to an infelicitous turn. Most probably, the privileges which he enjoyed at the seat of power resulted in eliciting the jealousy of the Maliki judges and other notable families of Cordoba. To appease them, al-Mansur found it prudent to exile him by sending him, in 1195, to a city south of Cordoba, Lucena. But after two years there, at the behest of the elite of Seville, Averroës returned to Marrakesh, where he died a few months later.[31]

Part three – directions taken by commentators regarding the "Decrees" of Ghazali and Averroës

In the introduction to his English translation of the *Decisive Treatise*, G. F. Hourani makes a signal contribution by clearly indicating its subject: Averroës' response to the challenged posed by Ghazali in his *Decisive criterion*.[32] He succeeds in renewing the debate among commentators, indeed, rendering it more pointed still, by highlighting the fact that Averroës wrote in his capacity as a "preeminent doctor of the law and judge" (as he put it himself) to ascertain the proper role of philosophical inquiry in Islam,[33] as Alain de Libera also noted in his introduction to the French translation of the *Decisive Treatise*.[34] The twentieth century debate has generally concerned itself with the rationalist posture of the *Commentator* (as medievals knew Averroës), which in their eyes had to cast suspicion on his orthodox Muslim faith.[35] But thanks to Hourani and de Libera, this possible tension between philosopher and judge surfaces at the heart of the *Decisive Treatise*, which Alain de Libera finds to be "the most representative text of the man and of his work."[36] For if the rapport between these two "sisters with the same nursing mother" – philosophy and revelation – is in fact harmonious, as the title of Hourani's English transition intimates, the same author also notes that the reasons for this harmony will escape an ordinary reader. So even if the source of Averroës' juridical rulings comes evidently from the existence of the inimitable book whose verses found the legal writ for philosophical inquiry in Islam, only philosophers can properly interpret these verses.[37] What is more, even if Averroës never held a "two-truth theory," as de Libera has clearly shown (nor, if I may be permitted to add, did Aristotle), it is still difficult to ascertain what revealed truth contributes to Averroës' properly philosophical activity.[38] This is an especially urgent question for those who, like Hourani, are unwilling to doubt his religious orthodoxy.[39]

It will become clear that the more Averroës argues for philosophers' preeminent role in interpreting the Qur'an, the more he seems to justify Ghazali's doubt whether he can identify any revealed truth which is essential to him as a philosopher. Moreover, this impression may remain even though he will not avoid knotty religious issues, like the mode of life proper to the afterlife,[40] in an effort to shed light on Ghazali's missteps, as we shall see in Chapter 4. So if we were to overlook the way Averroës manages, in the *Decisive Treatise*, never to contradict any of his "demonstrations" in elucidating his conception of the way revealed truth contributes to his philosophical activity,[41] we might readily conclude with Hourani that the *treatise* yields no positive indication on this subject.[42] Yet it remains to Hourani's credit that he directed anyone needing a response to these questions to a study of the properly philosophical works of Averroës: his commentary on the *Metaphysics* of Aristotle, as well as his original study of the terrestrial sphere, which we shall consider in the fifth chapter.

I am grateful for Hourani's counsel: that commentators need to be aware of the extreme character of Averroës' *Refutation of the Refutation*, a judgment reinforced by Barry Kogan.[43] This advice helps to spare us the error of Michel Allard, who used this work to account for any divergence between the Muslim commentator and Aristotle.[44] In any case it is clearly the idea of creation, giving testimony to the faith Averroës displays in an Artisan, which explains the divergence, if there be any. In his works reserved to philosophers, we can follow (as will become clear in Chapter 5) the path which distanced Averroës from a teleological view of nature, whereby the whole can move itself, to lead him better to appreciate how its unified existence rather displays a marvelous work of art, revealing the theological conception at work in this Muslim philosopher. Nevertheless, the relation between revelation and philosophy will be less of a "harmony" than a criss-crossing of emphases. From the viewpoint of the *Decisive Treatise*, only philosophers can interpret the Qur'an; from that of the commentator, only the certitude of faith in the existence of an Artisan can pinpoint the lacunae of Aristotle and show how to supplant them.

Nonetheless, it is clear that this second viewpoint, detailing the relation between the "two sisters" from the side of revelation, would be utterly superfluous to those like Marc Geoffroy, who identify Averroës' with effecting the "secularization of philosophy."[45] It would also be superfluous for one like Roger Arnaldez, who rightly calls attention to the central role the judge Averroës plays in the community, but is utterly convinced that he was in no way a religious thinker.[46] And while this point of view is quite secondary to those, like Majid Fakhry, who are quite certain of the commentator's acute originality, they nonetheless attribute it to the similarity of his thought to "the mathematical rationalism" of René Descartes.[47] Yet again, this perspective will allow us to surmount the judgment of I. A. Bello on the *Decisive Treatise*, where Averroës is seen to be an ingenious lawyer playing the innocent in linking himself to a mere pretext in order to exempt philosophers from the just accusations of Ghazali.[48]

Yet the following clarification is crucial: if the attitude of Averroës towards articles of faith must be evaluated from his philosophical works, and so be reserved to philosophers, that judgment will only exacerbate – if not scandalize – Ghazali, for whom these articles of faith must be accessible to any believer! So let us pass on to the *Decisive criterion*, where the religious orthodoxy and deep faith of the author has never been in doubt. Yet commentators diverge on the essential point of this short yet rich treatise. W. Montgomery Watt characterizes the *Decisive Criterion Distinguishing between Islam and the Hypocrites*[49] as a tract of dogmatic theology, in part directed against the *Batiniyya*, with the goal of defending Ghazali's own strategies for interpreting the Qur'an.[50] Richard Frank assesses the work in the light of Ghazali's general aim as an Ash'arite theologian intent on defending the "high theology" which he espouses.[51]

M. Hogga describes the work as a "complex yet important theological tract . . . examining modalities of judgment of unbelief by way of a veridical witness coextensive with five modes of existence."[52] He then goes on to note the specificity of this work in enlisting a "classificatory and repressive discourse" to help to re-align the community politically and religiously, under the aegis of the Abbasid-Seljuk polity.[53] By way of contrast, Sherman Jackson locates the specificity of this work in a way already noted by Ignace Goldziher, to be "a work uniquely devoted to the idea of tolerance."[54] Yet one wonders how this goal of tolerance could permit Ghazali to assure his own goal, clearly indicated by the title of this work: to distinguish Muslims from hypocrites, who cannot be authentic Muslims. I. A. Bello has identified the master-idea of the *Decisive criterion* in a way which links it directly to Ghazali's insistence that the articles of Muslim faith need no interpretation and must be taken literally.[55] Once that connection is made clear, we can see why the *qadi* of Cordoba, classified with the hypocrites by the spiritual master, Ghazali, must rectify so gross an error.

Yet we shall have to explain how the literal sense relates to the four other modes of existence, which apparently open a field of interpretation designed to assure that diverse theological currents remain within Islam. Jackson sees this intention guiding Ghazali, whereas sidelining philosophers with other hypocrites is purely secondary.[56] To this end he finds Ghazali introducing the idea of "a psychological prism proper to each learned interpreter of the Qur'an – all Muslims – who differ in their theological positions,"[57] thereby assuring his "ecumenism."[58]

Yet even if the goal of sidelining philosophers is only secondary, the way in which their "psychological prism" could be seen to distinguish them from Muslim rationalists is hardly clear. Nor does he clarify how the literal sense proper to articles of faith relates to the five degrees of existence in such a way as to assure their order of priority. Moreover, accentuating the idea of tolerance as central to the *Decisive criterion*, as does Goldzhiher, is at once surprising and astonishing in the light of a fact that Hava Lazarus-Yafeh already noted, and has now been reiterated by Martin Whittingham: that Ghazali here limits his focus to Muslims, never including believers as such.[59]

Finally, we will need to understand how Ghazali managed to assure the Muslim religious identity of both Sunni and Shi'ites. For distinguishing five modes of existence allowed him to admit divergent interpretations of the Qur'an while also revealing the hypocrisy of the philosophers. This will be the subject of Chapter Three.

Chapter 2

From the chimera of philosophy to the evidence of "*The Just Balance*"

Preamble

In her *Studies in al-Ghazali*, Hava Lazarus-Yafeh sums up fifteen years of scholarship devoted to the Arabic redaction of Ghazali's work, following the hypothesis of an intimate link between form and content in his work.[1] The results of this sustained inquiry were the prima facie surprising thesis that the style and vocabulary of Ghazali exhibit a remarkable stability.[2] Despite the considerable displacements in his life, she suggests that his vision of the world enjoyed, at root, an exceptional stability.[3] Her discovery confirms those commentators of Ghazali who had already underscored his lifelong faithfulness both to Ash'arism in theology and to the Shafi' school of Shari'a interpretation.[4]

Moreover, Lazarus-Yafeh even moves beyond this thesis, in situating the roots of this conceptual stability in Ghazai's unilateral motivation to offer spiritual direction to the Muslim community.[5] Yet direction of souls demands that one have a clear view of the goal to be attained, as well as of the obstacles, dangers and traps to avoid. Yet while the goal pursued by Ghazali was orthodox: to confirm believers in their assiduous practice of divine commands according to the Qur'an, his clear view of the principal trap to avoid was original. The trap was the more dangerous for its being deceptive, cloaking and concealing itself under what could seem to be the dignity proper to human beings endowed with reason. Called "philosophy," this trap reflects the pride and thirst for power leading human beings to their damnation.[6]

Now we must underscore at this point something which seems to have escaped the commentators: that Ghazali intended to oppose philosophy itself, and not simply counter one way of doing philosophy in the name of another which he would support. He expended his considerable oratorical and preaching talents to assure the salvation of his audience, from encouraging believers to engaging in irony to castigate those unfortunate enough to let themselves be convinced by the ruses and decoys employed by purveyors of falsehood.[7] Indeed, if we would properly appreciate the depth of his criticism of philosophy, we have only to attend to his insistence that the very term "philosophy" names a "pseudo-knowledge," as "philosophize" can only refer to a distorted use of the gift of reason. For Ghazali has nothing but esteem for the proper use of reason, as practiced by those engaged in exact sciences like mathematics and logic, as well as empirical sciences like astronomy, medicine and agriculture. Nor did he simply oppose philosophy proposed as a "mystique" reserved to an illuminated elite. Quite the contrary, he opposed it in the name of intelligent and critical Muslim believers, themselves inclined to acquire worthwhile knowledge in fields as diverse as logic and agriculture. It is this radical position which seems to have escaped commentators like Lazarus-Yafeh, for whom Ghazali could not be said to scorn philosophy because he appreciated the exact sciences and denigrated believers who neglected them.[8]

Yet the way we interpret an author whom we esteem often derives from our own vision of the world. In this same vein, Lazarus-Yafeh reproaches commentators of Ghazali who, relying on their own "enlightenment" education, fail to appreciate the value which Ghazali places on spiritual experience.[9] Yet her own shortcoming lies in having failed to discern that Ghazali does not use 'philosophy' to mean love of wisdom, but rather to denote the very heart of the moral fault of pride. Sayyed Mohammed Khatami, past president of the republic of Iran, evidenced the same misunderstanding when he queried why Ghazali had not rejected religion by the same argument he had used to reject philosophy: namely, that certain people had misused it?[10]

So it is crucial to realize that "philosophy" for Ghazali is neither a method nor a field of inquiry, but rather names the void attending the distorted use of reason constituting "philosophizing." From this perspective, there could be no significant difference between Plato, Plotinus or Aristotle, and all of their commentators, since they are all led astray by the chimera of "metaphysics," the heart of philosophy, which they assume is the pathway taken by those who think they are superior to others, to lead them to that precise point where logic enshrines the exquisite pinnacle of existence, the very point where being and knowledge unite.

This stance of Ghazali is rooted in his conviction that the sole source of any worthwhile content of thinking is that experience common to all human beings, who negotiate our unique world, quite aware of the impressions and sensation proper to each person. Experience alone, whether it be "objective" or "subjective," is at once necessary and sufficient for anyone wishing to progress in this life to the light of divine revelation in the Qur'an. So there can be nothing reserved to philosophers, who are after all pretentious and malign purveyors of falsehood, who intimidate their fellows in "closing the doors" and "blocking the way" before them.[11] Moreover, since there can be no categorical difference among human beings from the perspective of reason, there can hardly be any from the perspective of faith. So Lazarus-Yafeh contends: "I do not believe that Ghazali ever elaborated a theory or an esoteric truth."[12]

So human beings can only differ in degree, according to the intensity or the extent of their experience of the world about them, or stemming from the limpidity or right intention of their interior life. It is this radical equality among Muslims, all equally endowed with common sense, which leads Ghazali to contend that there is no need to conceive or construct a bridge between faith and reason, but one can simply address one's audience in the space forged by a faith informed by reason, and a reason fortified by faith, in which their experience is rooted.

This view of Ghazali will determine the order which I shall follow to explore his underlying intention in the three works considered, before and after his departure from Baghdad. The first part will be devoted to his introductions to the *Incoherence of the Philosophers*, where he expounds his view – contrary to that of Averroës – that there can be no connection between logic and metaphysics. In the second part I shall comment on Ghazali's introduction to the *Revivification of Religious Learning*, in the light of Book 28, devoted to the desire for power which holds human beings in its grip, so nicely highlighted by Farid Jabre.[13] And in the third part I shall employ *The Just Balance* to consider Ghazali's position regarding the logical rules which guide human beings endowed with common sense, as the Qur'an displays them.

Part one – logic and metaphysics

Michael Marmura's praise for the virtues of critical limpidity and ingenious reflection displayed by Ghazali in the *Incoherence of the Philosophers* is echoed by Marie-Louise Siauve. Marmura sees this work, by the director of the *Nizamiyya* in Baghdad, to have been composed to expose the scaffolding of the philosophical systems of Aristotle, al-Farabi (d. 950) and Avicenna (D. 1037): "an incomparable critique from the point of view of its range and its perspicacity";[14] or as Siauve puts it: "a pointed refutation displaying Ghazali's philosophy, whose power; seems to have escaped readers of the *Incoherence*."[15] This thrust of this ingenious critique is made clear in the preface and four introductions to this work. His objective was to confirm students and professors of the *Nizamiyya* in the Muslim faith by distancing them from the false incantations of philosophy. In the event, however, the vehemence and urgency to which he gives vent to show that philosophical systems can never reach a conclusion because they are nothing but houses of cards only held together by the vanity of their authors and the naiveté of their readers, offers poignant witness to the hope he once put in them, as well as to his own disillusion. Having already expounded the *Intentions of the Philosophers*, Ghazali now relies on his own experience to calculate the disastrous effect that they could have on students of the *Nizamiyya*, whose faith could only be weakened and easily overshadowed by the immense promise which these "great men" of antiquity parade before them.

Both al-Farabi and Avicenna entertained great hope in logic [*al-mantiq*], a term which in their eyes signified the intimate ties among thought, language, and reality.[16] Al-Farabi detailed three senses of this key term, explaining how it pertains to a capacity proper to human beings, allowing them to conceive eternal concepts, as well as the reciprocal relations among them, in a way which assures knowledge of existing things as well as of the distinction between good and evil.[17] So the relations among *being*, *true*, and *good* are clarified, as well as the fact that they are accessible to anyone who acquires *logic*. From this Avicenna inferred that logic is the key to a knowledge assuring human beings of the happiness and which they seek.[18]

In effect, he contends that Muslim commentators of Aristotle were persuaded that logic is at the heart of metaphysics, which itself assures eternal happiness by unfolding the exquisite criss-crossing of concepts which form the basis of beings leading to God Himself. Avicenna had even remarked that logic resembled God from this point of view, because it directs proper thought by leading it to happiness.[19] He also explained how human beings are not limited by their own languages since the objects which logic treats are *intelligible* concepts, whose meanings are transparent unities, carrying with them indication of their role in the structure of reality.[20] In this way, Avicenna defended the notion that logico-pilosophical inquiry is the only way towards human perfection and the most sure way of attaining happiness.

Indeed, one can only appreciate the proposals set forth in Ghazali's Preface (to the *Incoherence*) against the background of this immense hope, as he mocks the proud who are persuaded that they are endowed with superior intellectual capacities, distinguishing them for the rest of human beings.[21] Anyone recalling Avicenna's comparing logic to God would have to be sympathetic to the prayer Ghazali addresses to God, the

One who outreaches our comprehension, that He might incline us to know the True and the Good, and avoid lying and evil. Ghazali also addresses those in his audience who might be students of students of the great thinkers of antiquity. Concerning such "students of students," nothing authorizes them, mere imitators as they are, to neglect strict religious observance, as though they had moved beyond it. Indeed, the intellectual weakness of these "imitators" lies at the root of the doubts they instill, by dint of the esteem which the "important names" of scholars of antiquity inspire in them, by which they have come to believe that religious laws are mere human inventions.[22] The reasons they can take pride in their absence of faith can be traced to intellectual weakness and spiritual laziness. Ghazali not only considers that persons of this sort hardly qualify belonging to an intellectual elite, since they neither originate nor verify the ideas they have, but in their vanity end up vastly inferior to simple believers.[23]

In his first introduction, Ghazali explains why he prefers to focus on al-Farabi and Avicenna: to make clear that the immense esteem Muslim commentators of Aristotle enjoy is due to a misunderstanding.[24] That is, to have failed to distinguish between logic and metaphysics, a distinction which the very fact of many metaphysical systems should make evident. Failing to make that distinction, some are tempted to think we can prove the truth of a metaphysical system in ways similar to metaphysics or logic.

Now Ghazali's intention is to empty metaphysics itself of all significant content, once the aura of conclusive exactitude has been dispelled, thereby leaving its place open to theologians and Muslim jurists on the one hand, and practitioners of empirical science on the other. For in his second Introduction, Ghazali reduces the debate between theologians and philosophers between "creator" and "first substance" to a merely verbal one, since philosophers do not consider *substance* to be located in a place.[25] At the same time, wishing to nullify a vision of the world proper to Hellenistic philosophy, Ghazali sidesteps debates among Muslim theologians regarding the Creator's relation to space, even if it be His throne.[26]

Sidestepping divergences among diverse interpretations of the Qur'an (which he will let us find quite menacing to the unity of the Muslim community, as we shall see in Chapters Three and Four), Ghazali hopes here to highlight the difference between the accord uniting theologians and the disputes which divide philosophers. This accord among theologians allows him to conclude: "once specialists in Arabic have determined the sense of the formula 'what subsists in itself,'" all we need is a dictionary to ascertain whether we can use it to designate the Creator.[27] Yet given the fact that it is theologians and not jurists who are using the term "substance," we might surmise that there could be a significant difference between their respective domains, so introducing a division at the heart of the accord supposed to exist among those charged with elucidating the relation between God and human beings.

Yet Ghazali explains how any difference between the field proper to theologians and the competence of jurists can only be purely formal, because both have in mind "the true nature of things."[28] That is, both judges and theologians are concerned with the "licit," as it conforms to the true description of a thing which also serves as a rule of action. Yet it is experts in the sciences who concern themselves with the nature of things, it is not the office of theologians and jurists to do so. Indeed, given his audience of educated believers, students and professors of the *Nizamiiyya*, Ghazali has no intention of undermining the esteem they have for men of science, like astronomers who can foresee eclipses of sun and moon by accounting for them, yet at the same time he denies they have priority over theologians inn this regard. Distinguishing between formal sciences like geometry and arithmetic, operating with algorithms with specific rules of application, and empirical sciences confirmed by experience, he insists that hypotheses of empirical sciences can at best be well-justified suppositions. And this validates the superiority of theologians, since whatever the number of firmaments, the world is clearly the work of God.[29]

All of this clarifies the fundamental error of philosophers: by failing to elucidate the way reason can formulate hypotheses without being able to ground them, philosophers cannot appreciate the problematic state of their own field. Hence they can pretend to doubt articles of faith dealing with the temporal creation of the world, attributes of God, and resurrection of the body.[30] Nothing short of vanity can explain the fact – if it be a fact – that philosophers have come to deny the literal sense of these articles of faith, without ever being able to refute them.

In this third Introduction, Ghazali encourages both masters and students of theological schools to rally behind what unites them, to offer a united front in the face of their common enemy, philosophers divided. While carefully avoiding condemning philosophers as wrongdoers, he bolsters his audience with a sense of impatience which their manner of considering themselves superior to ordinary mortals cannot but awaken in others, which becomes the subject of his fourth Introduction.[31] He emphasizes that there can be no possible justification allowing anyone to employ logic so as to perceive truths hidden to someone else. As a result, Ghazali also emphasizes that philosophers have avoided any acknowledgement of their wrongdoing.[32]

Yet this very ambiguity explains why he will hesitate in the end to describe philosophers as renegades.[33] Of course, a judgment of that sort would have to leave room for the conviction shared among Muslims, and at the very heart of different theological positions, which would exceed the bounds of the *Incoherence of the philosophers*. This subject will be treated in our third chapter, devoted to issues raised in the *Decisive criterion*. As he notes explicitly in concluding the *Incoherence*,[34] he prefers to stay within the limits here imposed, rather than take up questions which could require that "heretical innovators," like those aligned with the Mu'tazailites, be identified as infidels.[35] The burden of the *Incoherence* asks only that Ghazali elucidate the groundless pride of philosophers who unwarrantedly celebrate the coherence of their strategies of inquiry. He is intimately convinced that nothing at all could confirm intellectual superiority in certain human beings. Philosophers who pretend they are superior actually show themselves to be similar to everyone by their way their own pride has overtaken them. That will be the subject of the following section.

Part two – the heart of human beings and its desire for power

The invective Ghazali directs to proud philosophers and those naïve enough to be seduced by them is a small thing in comparison to his attack on Muslim judges (*qadi*'s) and theologians in his Introduction to the *Revivification of Religious Learning*. Once he had terminated his brilliant career at the *Nizamiyya* in Baghdad, he became clear-sighted about this pseudo-elite, in which he had until quite recently played a stellar role: composed of people with no other thought in mind than their power and earthly success, they and their epigones had plenty of ways to assure their domination. They are even more responsible for alienating people from their faith than the philosophers of antiquity, because they had uprooted themselves from their very identity:

> as a result, the allure of religious learning is tarnished, like a torch of truth and guidance from one end of the earth to another. People are brought to think that knowledge is nothing but a *fatwa* [a religious decree], to which judges and legal scholars have recourse, or else the dialectic which ambitious people don to dominate others by reducing them to silence.[36]

It should be clear that this contention of a generally unfavorable state of affairs goes hand in and with Ghazali's bitterly acute awareness of his own vanity. For that very vanity had consolidated his role at the heart of the Abbasso-Saljuk dynasty, led him to believe that theologians and jurisprudents were at one with each other, and so to be distinguished from philosophers divided among themselves, and finally and crucially, a vanity which had obscured his own hypocrisy from himself. For though he had followed the voice of the ancient commentators of Aristotle in order to silence it in their writings, he had not had the courage to adopt his own philosopher. His refutation of philosophy had been oriented by a vision of the world, together with everything happening in it, as founded uniquely on the will of God, who is the only agent. God creates the world and with it time and space. This act emanates from the absolute power of bringing forth existence and what does not exist. Absolutely free, God is the only true agent.

Nevertheless, Ghazali was unable to renounce his own will; notably, entertaining the illusion that he could choose from among many paths the one which best suited him. In examining his own soul, he was persuaded that illusion with regard to many paths had to be a ruse of the devil. For in fact, there is only one choice: to seek the goal which had been his ephemeral glory for himself; or carry out the will of God for the sole reason that it is His will. Ghazali detailed this discovery in his *Deliverance from Error*:

> I reflected on my actions – of which teaching was the best – only to see that my studies were futile. . . . Moreover, what was my goal in proffering my teaching? My intention was hardly pure; it was not oriented to God. Was not my impulse rather to gain glory and renown? I stood posed on a precipice; if I did not step back, I was going to fall into the Fire.[37]

In composing the *Revivification of Religious Learning*, the spiritual master, Ghazali, had his own identity as a Muslim in view, as well as that of his Muslim brethren:

> since this [deplorable situation] represents a pernicious fissure in religion, as well as a somber and baleful event, I became aware of the importance of writing this book, as a way of putting life back into religious learning . . ., of restoring the path of the ancient guides, and letting useful knowledge flourish. . . .[38]

The forty books of this work are designed to delineate different facets of the daily life of those who are taking the path towards the only worthwhile goal: to do the will of the utterly Other who is God. Subject to the blinding light of this goal of finding one's proper place before God – that is, one of a servant who accomplishes the orders of the Master because he so wills them – that human beings learn what really belongs to them: their own desire to dominate. Assiduous reading of the Qur'an, together with an examination of conscience, will unveil the multiple ruses used by believers to fulfill God's commandments for motives of their own. We must emphasize that this endeavor to revitalize the roots of religion has nothing esoteric about it, nor does Ghazali's teaching as a spiritual guide contain any revelations directed to an elite minority. Ghazali has no desire to give support to the way of mystical unveiling, but rather to contribute to the way of practice and religious rules by rooting them in a renewed intention of a believer to undertake doing the will of God: "reason needs above all to address itself to the soul, laying down duties and conditions to indicate the way to the good, as well as putting it in order to follow them. Finally reason can never let up its control over the soul, even for an instant."[39]

Ghazali insists on the duty of gratitude to God, the unique source of all that exists, noting that religious obligations only give witness to the believer's recognition: "Bodily actions in prayer express gratitude for the body which He has given us, becoming the alms in recognition of the goods which He bestows on us."[40] Faith itself is but the patient endurance sustaining the daily struggle of believers to articulate their awareness of God, the unique source of all that is. Everything depends on the intention of the believer and everything returns to God, the unique agent and absolutely free master. So a long journey, never finished here below, opens before believers, where the evidence of absolute freedom, which pertains to God alone, emerges once they realize their own captivity, in the light of their examination of conscience. This twofold perspective inspires one to abandon oneself to God [*tawakkul*], as a corollary to the principle of divine unicity [*tawhid*], which he treats in Book 39 of the *Revivification*, eliciting an anguish peculiar to this Muslim believer, al-Ghazali. For believers must not merely accept passively God's will for them, but must exercise constant control over their acts, as well as account for all their thoughts while examining their intentions. So in one way all returns to God, so the anguish of Ghazali hardly corresponds to that of a Paschal or a Kierkegaard, as Marie-Louise Siauve indicates: "it is in no way anguish over a decision made in darkness, but rather an anguish attending our ignorance of the choice which God has made for us."[41] His is also the anguish attending someone who cannot resist knowing the hold which his own will to power exerts over him, as a fresh examination of conscience reminds him.

This twofold anguish accompanies the certitude attending Ghazali's comprehension of the Word of God in the Qur'an, which will be the subject of our third chapter. In effect, the more believers enter into the absoluteness of God's commands, as well as the ineluctable character of the last judgment, the deeper is one's anguish not to know the choice God has made for them, especially when they know how far they are from the place which should be theirs, of servant of God, the only Master.

Farid Jabre admirably succeeds to illuminate the depth of the somber side of a radical equality among human beings, all called to become servants God yet all equally in the grip of their will to power. This is the subject of our second chapter, devoted to the psychological substratum in which *tawakkul* and *tawhid* – abandoning oneself to God, the sole Master – will have to be rooted.[42]

What is cunning about this will to power, as a constitutive inclination of the human heart, is the intimate way it is linked with everything that seems to undergird our fundamental dignity as creatures called to become loving servants of God:

> In the human heart lies an inclination towards the quality of sovereignty.... It is by virtue of something "sovereign" in them that human beings naturally love sovereignty; a sense of sovereignty stemming from the unique way in which we possess perfection and existence. For perfection pertains to divine qualities as well, which brings human beings to love it. Indeed, perfection *tout court* is the fact of being unique in existence ... So every human being naturally loves to be the one to possess perfection. ... Yet perfection consists in dominating over all things that exist. ... So dominating over everything becomes, quite naturally, something lovable because it is a kind of perfection. ...[43]

So human beings come to realize they are their own worst enemies, alienated from the goal of becoming servants of God, like other creatures. Called to fulfill the divine will, believers grow in their awareness that God's sovereignty is absolute. In this way, they will realize better and better that only God, the unique master, all powerful and free, can be the object of a love able to fill whatever is best in human creatures, that is, their thirst for perfection. Yet, like Tantalus, this very thirst for perfection which believers desire to realize for themselves is the very thing which keeps them from imbibing it. Called to become servant of God, believers must begin by accepting their place among those equally chained like them to the desire for vanity. So the only way for believers to progress along the path of *tawhid* and *tawwakul* will be by virtue of daily fidelity to practice of the commands of God, in the light of the acute awareness they will attain from [attending to] the yawning gap between their own intentions and the only one necessary: to engage in the practices they do for the sole reason that it is the will of God.

Indeed, the fact that all believers, participating in daily practices together, are equally equipped to find their way allows Ghazali to show (in his *Just Balance*) how common sense and a literal sense of Qur'anic revelation criss-cross, which we shall elucidate in the following section.

Part three – the evidence of experience in *The Just Balance*

Ghazali himself gives decided prominence to the treatise he composed at the end of his extended period of retreat, *The Just Balance*,[44] for these "nearly twenty fascicules" contain five rules which are the sure criteria of all truth.[45] He conceived these five rules, as "norms of truth, faithful instruments of measure, and criteria of exact weight," to bring sterile debates over interpreting the revelation of God in the Qur'an to an end.[46] These discussions found various partisans of rational argument opposed to one another, on the one hand, with followers of an infallible imam; that is to say, the *Batiniyya*, on the other.

This treatise will illuminate for us the basic disagreement between Ghazali and Averroës, both of whom find themselves opposed to the *Batiniyya*, but for opposite reasons. Ghazali, for whom God can never lead his servants astray, deems that everyone is equally able to understand the sense of revelation; while Averroës is rather convinced that philosophers alone are in a position to understand he veridical and coherent whole which is revelation. These two positions, whose course we shall pursue in the third and fourth chapters, provide the grids structuring the contrasting readings of the Qur'an which our authors will propose.

The Just Balance has the advantage of conveying the very root of the conception of truth which Ghazali finds accessible to everyone. As spiritual guide, he has become convinced of the gap between the intention which faithful should have and the one which actually motivates them; and intimately persuaded, as well, that there can be no significant difference among human beings, who are all endowed with reason and so able to understand Qur'anic revelation. For if that were not the case, or were we to accept that God could in fact mislead his servants, then no interpretation supposedly based on the literal sense yet propounded to deepen and enrich the sensibility of the faithful, would clearly differ from allegory, so every spiritual guide would *ipso facto* assume the soul of poet. Yet it may be that the immense respect Ghazali enjoys among commentators could befog and impede a clear grasp of his conceptions here, notably of the peculiar way he employs the term "syllogism," in expounding his five rules of truth. For Hogga, *The Just Balance* postulates a "correspondence between Qur'anic argumentation and Greek syllogistic, or formal logic."[47] For M-L. Siauve, this treatise permits us to perceive the originality of Ghazali's method, which "like the celebrated Cartesian method . . . makes orderly progress from the simple to the composite."[48]

But these flattering depictions hardly square with Ghazali's intent of dislodging philosophers from the place they pretend to occupy by dint of the excellence of reason. For in *The Just Balance* he wants to make room for his position regarding the rules for the proper use of reason in the world submissive to the benevolent will of God. But such role would be one of induction; so Ghazali refuses to grant reason any excellence, if it be reason according to Aristotle. Validity of syllogisms can in no way be a formal one for him, but is rather due to their content as it reflects the order of the forms at the foundation of the intelligibility of nature. He would also deny any validity to reason according to Descartes, for whom reason is the ability to affirm clear and distinct ideas, an activity proper to God, at work in a world once whirlpools replace Aristotle's natural substances.

In *The Just Balance*, far from such proud and profoundly erroneous notions, Ghazali sets out to safeguard at once the absolute transcendence of God, the sole agent, as well as a radical equality among believers. By addressing Shi'ite "strangers" whom he would have met on his pilgrimage, disciples of the *Batiniyya*, he is also able to speak to all Muslim convinced that the Qur'an is the complete and veridical revelation of God to the last of the prophets.[49]

Now disciples of the *Batiniyya* are as convinced as Ghazali of this last fundamental truth, yet they go on to insist that none but the perfect and infallible imam can guide believers in Qur'an interpretation. Yet without the twin conviction which offers the key to the originality of *The Just Balance*, Ghazali's dialogue with the stranger would have quickly been derailed. One the one hand, as a believing Muslim, the stranger could not fail to admit that as the word of God, the Qur'an is master and guide. Yet on the other hand, he would have to deny what Ghazali wants him to admit: that the same rules of truth guide every human being endowed with common sense – the stranger himself as well as his imam – and that they are contained in the Qur'an itself. So Ghazali foregrounds the common sense with which all believers are endowed, making note of the fact that he derives this teaching from the free revelation of the creator and sole master who calls human beings to be his servants. So the sole master of Muslims is the Qur'an, whose verse "weight with a just balance" (17:35) serves as the title for this treatise.

But what is the criterion for authentic knowledge? Ghazali explains that it lies in the correspondence between a particular sensible given and the general rule established by recurrent experience.[50] So how, then, can one determine whether the set of scales which one has just bought, or the one the merchant uses, are just? Ghazali reminds the stranger that answering this question requires neither scientific competence nor the advice of artisans. It is enough to note that both trays are at the same level when the pointer is perpendicular.[51] The quite special syllogism which Ghazali presents displays the results of correspondence between an experimental and a general premise – two trays where the weight is equal, together with a perpendicular pointer at the same level – along with an equally experimental particular premise regarding the set of scales one is observing, from which one concludes that this set of scales is just. Moreover, note how utterly humble a syllogism this is: not a hint of the depth of one's experience, nor of the way our experience might participate in the intention of the good God who so wills things to be.

Moreover, the Qur'an appeals to such a correspondence when Abraham, wanting to persuade Nimrod that he was not god, said to him: "God makes the sun rise in the east and set in the west." Then from that general experience he returns Nimrod to his own experience: "It is hardly Nimrod who makes the sun rise." From these two premises we can conclude that Nimrod is not God.[52]

So disciples of the *Batiniyya* are given a choice, neither of whose terms are desirable: either to deny that induction is in fact our best guide in daily life, or to insist that the ultimate meaning of Qur'anic revelation has nothing at all to do with what assures the course of the world and its perdurance. Yet since the stranger's infallible imam remains human, he would hardly want him to be utterly alien to the rules of common sense we all share. Moreover, given the very excellence of the absolute meaning of the revelation of God, no one would want to question its connection with daily human life. So in the face of this doubly undesirable consequence, Ghazali can presume that the stranger will accept the rule of equivalence displayed in comparing particular with general experience, a rule as intimately implicated in the Word of God addressed to human beings to become servants, the Qur'an itself, as it is in human daily life.

This rule of equivalence is presented as the first of five criteria of truth.[53] The second (or "middle") rule is also expressed by Abraham in the Qur'an (6:76), when he remarks about the stars: "I do not like things that disappear."[54] The ostensible meaning of this verse is that there is an absolute dichotomy between the perpetually active presence of God, and all that is not God. The third (or "small") rule shows the impossibility of articulating a general rule if it be contradicted by a particular fact.[55] What makes this rule especially interesting is the way it illustrates once again the profound difference between an Aristotelian syllogism and the kind Ghazali proposes. Faced with a particular being whose movement apparently contradicted that of the essence to which it presumably belongs, Aristotle would have inferred an error in identification rather than doubting the "general," for it pertains to the essence of the entity in question: should a fish not swim, either it is sick or is not a fish. Whereas for Ghazali, the particular experience of believers takes precedence; only unbelievers would say that "God has revealed nothing to mortals" (6:91). So general an assertion could never be countenanced, for Moses, moral though he was, had the law revealed to him.

The two last rules, those of necessary consequence and of opposition, serve to enhance the weight given to experiential facts, by way of forestalling any possible doubts as well as overcoming any attempt at explanation. Necessary consequence amounts to noting that once one has eaten they are satisfied. Similarly with opposition, should anyone enter a duplex, if he is not in one part of the house, he will conclude that he is in the other.

In the end, it seems clear to me that Ghazali, in becoming spiritual master, displays his utter originality in elucidating the power and worth of a logic which has no connection whatsoever with the presumption of philosophers nor the credulity of the *Batiniyya*. This logic is based on the common sense of believers as they face Qur'anic revelation, so it will be in that light that I propose reading the *Decisive Criterion* in the chapter to come.

Chapter 3

The decisive criterion of the distinction between Islam and hypocrisy (zandaqa)

Preamble

Returning to his academic role in Nishapur, at the end of 1105, Ghazali is now a spiritual master, strengthened by years of retreat which led him to sharpen his view of things, giving him the ability to distinguish Muslim believers from those who call themselves people of faith.[1] This new ability filled him with a fresh goal, as he confesses: "I felt myself able to unravel these ambiguities, as unmasking such people became easier than drinking a glass of water."[2]

If we are to read his text, however, we need to be apprised of specific features of the Muslim community which Ghazali sought to purify. As continues to be true today, the Qur'an was the base of all intellectual, ethical and legal reflection, yet his community was set apart by their overweening confidence in Islamic sovereignty, with its attendant cultural superiority. For all that, however, it was threatened from within by the despotism which some judges, theologians, and philosophers exerted over ordinary believers, doing so by virtue of their purported superiority as interpreters of the Qur'an. So the *nahda* [renaissance] which he envisaged as spiritual master had to come from within, revivifying believers' certitude regarding God's existence, as well as their radical equality as servants.

This background helps to articulate Ghazali's dual project in the *Decisive Criterion*. His first motive is to fend off a danger threatening believers' religious identity, resulting from the presence of a self-styled pious cohort of proud hypocrites, convinced of their own superiority, especially as Qur'an interpreters. His second motive is to bring people to recognize the clear superiority which is his: an ability to encourage believers to a quality of self-examination designed to bolster the primacy of the spiritual master in their midst. These intentions are intimately linked:

hypocrites will not be unmasked without the sage advice of a spiritual master, who in turn will be unable to fulfill such a role unless the community recognizes how much it needs his singular insight.

Nothing can threaten the Muslim community other than the bad faith of a few. Once Sherman Jackson had noted this fact, in the introduction to his English translation of this treatise, it became clear to me that "hypocrite" best rendered the term *zandaqa* in the title of this chapter.[3] In his translation, Jackson renders it "masked infidelity," Yet he suggests "hypocrisy" himself when he cites the Hanbalite author, Ibn Qudama (d. 1223), to note how "religious hypocrisy," translated by *nifaq* in the time of the Prophet, had become *zandaqa* by Ghazali's time.[4]

But how are we to recognize hypocrites clever enough to threaten Muslims in their inmost selves, that is, their personal identity as believers? How are we to unmask them so as to exclude them from the cover they enjoy as part of the circle of Qur'an interpreters? Ghazali will have recourse to strong medicine: fear of our final ends, subject to the judgment God will render with the hope it can elicit. On his return to public life, he will put into play a theme which already structured the thirty-third book of the *Revivification*.[5]

With the difference, however, that during his retreat, this theme had been forcibly linked with his desire to awaken believers by enlivening the roots of their faith, to help them return to the intention which must be theirs: to engage in practices of piety solely because God so wills it. Aware that believers remain infinitely distant from this goal, as any examination of conscience will reveal, as well as hoping to distinguish believers from unbelievers, he foregrounds the specific way in which believers must live in time: by fear and by hope. Now many degrees of fear and hope can be found, with a huge chasm between ordinary faithful and those celebrated in the Qur'an: "the most noble among you before God are those with most fear" (49:13). Most noble are those who no longer fear punishment, but whose fear stems from their awareness of the utter insignificance of human beings before the supreme grandeur of God; those who no longer dread the fire of hell but rather the veil which their own will interposes between them and God.[6] Nevertheless, for most believers, fear of punishment with the hope of being spared is intermingled with fear of not knowing God's decision, to the point where believers who would not fear God could not be said to believe. Ghazali insists that fear of God is at once a duty and a condition of faith.[7]

Might one identify the fear which Ghazali commends with that of any believer, as Jackson seems to espouse, when he refers to the "ecumenical dimension" of the *Decisive Criterion*,[8] or even a purely human fear: "in human society there is ultimately no more powerful a position than that of being just human?"[9] Yet that cannot be what Ghazali has in mind here, for his goal is to make believers into just Muslims, where "just" comprises those who avoid what is forbidden, as well as anything which, though not expressly forbidden, either could lead to impurity or fail to conform to the scrupulous application of the commands of God in the Qur'an.[10] So the criterion decisively distinguishing Islam from hypocrisy will be the razor's edge of fear, which will serve as a sure criterion since hypocrites generally think they are best, resting confident in the intellectual and spiritual superiority they claim for themselves.

All this suggests the order which my interpretation of the *Decisive Criterion* will follow. The first section will be devoted to the primary place given to the first degree of existence, that of the literal sense, which denotes existence as apprehended by all human beings endowed with common sense, according to the five-fold disposition Ghazali proposes for interpreting the Qur'an. The second section will focus on the examples Ghazali chooses to illustrate inappropriate uses of the strategies proposed, foregrounding the roles played by fear of judgment and the radical equality of believers, to distinguish them from hypocrites. Here the space Ghazali has opened for various interpretations of the precious Book will be eclipsed by the duty of a truly believing interpreter, who must never forget that theoretical disagreements are quite secondary; the sole essential being a fear which begets hope and mercy – a subject which we shall address in the sixth chapter.

Part one – how the first degree of existence is present in the other four

The five-fold strategy Ghazali proposes for interpreting the Qur'an has the advantage of addressing the many disparate goals that he purportedly has in mind. First of all, this theory of interpreting is intended for the precious book alone, so is directed to Muslims in their legal status as believers. Yet within the Muslim community, this strategy of emphasizing the shared conviction of critical and intelligent believers in the truthfulness of the verses of the Qur'an, can also assure a space for divergences among them. Finally, the rules of proper use of the strategy help to diminish the meaning of such divergences among Qur'an interpreters, while underscoring the fact that hypocrites cannot employ this strategy. As a consequence, while the boundary separating Muslims from non-believers remains a legal affair, the truly significant boundary will be a completely interior one, visible only to a spiritual guide who can discern it in order to ferret out hypocrites. For given a clear definition of unbelief, Ghazali explains how there can be no unbelievers in the community of Islam "so long as they remain firmly attached to the witness that there is no god but God, and that Muhammad is his Messenger" (B92, C19).[11]

So properly speaking, unbelief only pertains to "others" found outside the frontiers of the Islamic empire: "Unbelief [*kufr*] is to deem anything the Prophet brought to be a lie, [while] 'faith [*îmân*]' is to deem everything he brought to be true" (B92, C19). Here the variety of unbelievers, all destined to the same end, is contrasted with the solidarity of those gathered together by the perspicuous Word into the assembly of believing Muslims.

> So Jews and Christians are unbelievers . . ., 'deists' [*Barâhima*] are *a fortiori* unbelievers, . . ., as are atheists. . . . For like slavery and freedom . . ., 'unbelief' is a legal designation, so sanctioning death for those guilty of it, as well as bringing the sanction of everlasting fire . . .
>
> (B92, C19)

The end uniquely reserved to unbelievers corresponds to the fault they all share: accusing the Messenger of lying; while the attitude of Muslims by contrast, to acknowledge the truthfulness of everything the Messenger has transmitted, is based in the distinction Ghazali proposes among five modes of existence.

Yet we must note how he lists these modes as though they embodied clear distinctions which everyone knows. "In fact, existence may be particular [*dhâti*, which M. Hogga renders 'essential' while Jackson uses 'ontological'], or sensible, or imagined ['imaginaire' for Hogga], or rational, or analogous [(*shabahi*), that is 'metaphorical' for Hogga]" (B94, C22). We shall see how the summary explication following the list emphasizes the unproblematic character of these modes of existence, appealing as it does to experience common to all human beings when they perceive beings in the world and are conscious of those experience, all equally real for those experiencing them. Yet before any explication, Ghazali clarifies what is essential to all the modes: they all allow believers to affirm the truthfulness of everything the Messenger asserts: "whoever recognizes the existence of what the Messenger (may God bless him) asserts to be under one of these five modes cannot accuse him of lying" (B94, C22). Note, however, as we shall see, that far from opening a space in which Muslims might diverge at the heart of their faith, the five-fold strategy rather leads to unifying them, thanks to anchoring the modes of existence in the first and plain sense. For the themes transmitted by the

Messenger regard facts and gestures belonging to human beings like us, in such a way as to presume that everything in existence depends totally on the will of God. Whoever attests to the truthfulness of everything which the Messenger communicates does so first by apprehending all the objective things constituting the world common to us all, which extends, Ghazali insists, to heaven, earth, animals and plants, all of whom are gathered up in the first mode of existence. Moreover, he notes that "as the most known mode of existing, most human beings never attribute any other meaning to existence" (B94, C22).

So the first mode of existence constitutes the objective domain of the real, in which all our perceptions are anchored. The second mode includes the awareness proper to human beings who inhabit this shared world. Yet Ghazali does not linger over "subjective" difference, but emphasizes their common aspects. For he includes in this second mode what human beings commonly see when awake, as well as what appears to them in sleep, and even visions proper to prophets. What all these intentional contents have in common is that they are as real as they are evident, so testifying, for those who experience them, to what is.

So if the primary mode of existing belongs to existence in its objective dimension, the second represents existence in its subjective dimension, without, however, subjecting it to evaluation. Dreams of the simple believer are as much tokens of this second order as images "comparable to the substance of the angels by whom revelation and inspiration are transmitted to prophets and saints" (B94, C22). It is hardly necessary to emphasize that this cannot be presented as a philosophical theory reserved to an elite. The second mode of existence intends to embrace the range of subjective points of view which belong to human beings as such. Regarding the third mode, Ghazali makes clear that it has to do with perduring representations of real things, whether things themselves – like horses or elephants – disappear when one closes one's eyes or not (B95, C23). So the third mode elucidates how subjective contents, like images, are anchored in the objectively real, as in the first mode of existence. As for the fourth mode of existence, it is concerned with meanings and the content of definitions. So a hand, for example, can signify "the ability to seize and strike," where that ability is associated with the hand, rationally apprehended (B95, C23). This mode of existence will also include capacities for action whose reality is not so strictly tied to sensible forms which we know. So "seizing and striking" need not be related to a human hand, nor must a pen, as instrument for preserving and transmitting the sciences, be made of wood. So the fourth mode of existence shows how specific things, understood in the first sense of existence, constitute an active set. The objectively real is hardly inert, but is a set of events which concern and affect us even though we may not be able to master these capacities nor understand the intentions motivating them.

The fifth mode of existence will confirm that fact that the five-fold strategy does not display ontological distinctions. "Analogous" or "metaphorical" do not refer to a specific mode of existing, but rather to a rapport among existing things such that something less known may become known through the name signifying a better known thing. By this rapport we can highlight an attribute of one being without attending to other attributes, which we do whenever we call a human being a "savage wolf," thereby highlighting one's ferocity without attending to their eloquence. So we are reminded that this rapport already licensed us to use the word "hand" to signify an ability to seize and strike, without implying a flesh and blood member of the body, so we need not ask how many fingers has the "hand of God," when speaking of God's ability to exercise force.

According to Ghazali, this fifth mode becomes especially valuable for interpreting the Qur'an allegorically, and even more precisely to account for God's unique agency. In effect, beings existing according to the first mode can act only by virtue of their rapport with the One unique agent, nor could we account for spiritual attributes and perfections, signified by God's ninety-nine names, without attending to His absolute transcendence, including His active willing. In elucidating the fifth mode, Ghazali emphasizes that it

> applies to an object existing neither in external shape nor in essence, neither in external nor internal senses, neither in imagination nor in reason; so that what exists in this way is other than what resembles it by one of its characteristics or attributes.
>
> (B95, C23)

Returning to this subject later, Ghazali shows how this fifth mode allows interpreters to plumb the meaning of divine attributes like "anger, passion, joy, and patience." He focuses on God's anger since it is intimately linked with his vision regarding the will of God as the ultimate reason for all that takes place, including our unhappiness and suffering (B100, C28).

> Whoever succeeds in demonstrating the impossibility of anger in God . . . will interpret anger to refer to some other attribute which produces the same *result* as anger, such as the will to punish. But this will

does not correspond to the essential reality of anger, but only to one of its attributes: . . . the fact of inflicting pain.

(B100, C28)

In this way, the fifth mode protects the absolute transcendence of God, the meaning of dire events as products of a will rather than mere chance, together with the reality of our experiences in the second mode of existence.

So we may conclude that Ghazali's account of the five-fold strategy clearly attests to the primacy of the first mode, the plain sense, the one most known to human beings endowed with common sense. I would also suggest that this first sense will distance hypocrites from the community of Qur'an interpreters, whose truthfulness will be confirmed with the help of Ghazali's approach. This is the case since hypocrites – be they philosophers or some Sufis – typically think that they alone can decipher the true sense of existence. Yet all they would have to do is to construct an interpretative grid based on that common sense which focuses each of the other modes.

Note how well this suggestion displays a firm link connecting the five-fold strategy with the decisive criterion distinguishing Islam from hypocrites, thereby assuring from the outset a way of purifying the set of Qur'an interpreters, without needing to examine the meaning which certain hypocrites will give to fundamental principles of faith, like "the resurrection of the body and the physical reality of sufferings in the next world," whose plain sense can hardly be altered without being accused of unbelief (B109, C39). So hypocrites will have to acknowledge the immense distance separating them from Muslim interpreters of Qur'anic revelation well before becoming the object of legal condemnation themselves. Now the primacy of the first mode of existence will also allow one to respond to a question which the law governing the use of the fivefold strategy could well raise, which he treats in section eight (B108, C33). Ghazali presents this law as the result of a fundamental agreement among Qur'an interpreters.

Now listen to the law of allegorical interpretation: . . . all concur in subordinating the exercise of allegorical interpretation to having demonstrated the impossibility of a plain meaning. The first literal sense . . . embraces all other modes of existence, but when it fails, we have recourse to sensible existence, so that if we can affirm this, it will embrace the modes which follow. If not, we will have recourse to imaginative or rational existence, and only when these cannot obtain will we finally turn to metaphorical or figurative existence.

(B108, C33)

This law of allegorical interpretation emphasizes the role of negative demonstration regarding the impossibility of certain meanings, according to a descending order of inclusion following the five modes. But the law itself hardly explains why philosopher hypocrites could not claim a legitimate place among allegorical interpreters. Without the presumption of the primacy the first mode of existence plays in affirming truth according to each of the modes, philosophers could maintain that everything the Messenger transmitted was allegorical. A hypocrite like that would insist that none of these things could resemble what is apparent to us: God's very existence, or what sort of bodies, or punishments and rewards, will be ours in the next world; as well as the very anger of God. Indeed, their conviction of the absolute transcendence of God should keep a place for philosophers among believers. But what serves to ferret out the deceptions of the proud is evidence that the first sense of existence provides the ultimate foundation, yielding the plain meaning known to most people (B94, C22). Moreover, this same pride lies at the root of the insouciance some hypocrites profess regarding their own destiny in the world to come. Yet in the examples he employs to illustrate the proper use of the fivefold strategy of interpretation, Ghazali focuses on this destiny, as the object of fear and hope of believers endowed with common sense. Yet the proud, who insist on boasting of their disinterest and detachment from the sensible in the name of their superiority, have no fear at all.

Part two – blessed are those who fear . . .

Ghazali devotes section five of his *Decisive Criterion* to examples suggesting how to apply the proposed strategy to interpreting (B93–96, C25–29). As we have insisted, this interpretative theory is proposed for believing Muslims. Outside a shared faith, it would be a dead letter, utterly opaque to anyone who failing to participate in the subjectivity of believers. We have noted how the first mode denominates real existence, objective and autonomous, on which sense and reason depend. Yet his interpretation presumes a point of view which regards this as a stupendous work, evoking the marvel and astonishment of believers reminded of their total dependence on the will of God, the sole agent and judge. Outside this perspective which sustains and circumscribes the subjectivity shared by believers, no experience makes sense, whether it be waking or sleeping, or the inspirations received by prophets and saints. Ghazali foregrounds this fact in proposing examples of the first mode of existence that are so well known to inhabitants of the house of faith that he thinks them "to be superfluous" (B96, C25). For it is what is understood by its evident form and needs no interpretation: true and absolute existence, such as what the Messenger – may God bless him – announced, regarding the Throne ['arsh], the Seat [kursî], and the Seven Heavens. These are to be taken in their plain meaning, without interpretation, since they are corporeal entities existing in their own right, whether perceived or not by sense or imagination.

(B96, C25)

Yet these bodies certainly differ from mortal bodies of animals or plants, which Ghazali had proposed as paradigms of the first mode of existence, "the best known" and that to which most human beings attribute the notion of existence (B94, C22).

In any case, anyone unfamiliar with the way the Living, the Awakened, the Creator, the all-powerful Judge with his Throne, are intimately linked to our destiny could not fail to note the chasm separating the Throne from the visible and palpable existence of the contingent things surrounding us. Yet this link is at the heart of Muslim faith. So the three following quotations must be directed to Jews and Christians, "peoples of the Book," potential readers of this inquiry, since they would be transparently clear to Muslims:

God, there is none but He, the alive, the ever real. Slumber takes him not, nor sleep. Everything in the heavens and the earth is His, and who – His leave apart – shall intercede with Him? He knows everything that mankind have presently in hand, and everything about them that is yet to be. Of a knowledge like His they are entirely uncomprehending – unless He gives them leave to know. In the vastness of the heavens and the earth his throne is established. Tirelessly He preserves them. So great is His majesty.

(2:255)

Put your trust in the living One who dies not, and celebrate his praise. He is full well aware of his servants' sin – He who created the heavens and the earth in six days and then seated himself on the Throne, the merciful One. Concerning Him, question a source that knows.

(25:60)

Relentless indeed is your Lord's power. He it is who brings into being and brings again anew. He is the One who forgives and who loves, the glorious Lord of the Throne.

(85:12–15)

Ghazali proposes the two examples of proper use of the grid of interpreta-tion to believers who dwell in certitudes like these. Recalling how this mode encompasses all of our perceptions, we will realize that it limns the contours of our very life. That is, the life of believers, which extends from the temporal life that is ours now to that constant and infinitely more meaningful life which will be ours on that day which resembles no other, when death will be overcome and the incomparable realities of paradise and of hellfire will appear. It is this background which sustains Ghazali's two examples: "first, a saying of the Messenger, may God bless him: 'on the last Day, they will bring a speckled ram to slaughter between paradise and hellfire'" (B97, C25).

As Ghazali makes clear, it matters little how this saying is interpreted, so long as we hold fast to the truth of what is said: "that the people who are present on the Day of Judgment will see this event and believe that the slaughtered animal is death. This, however, will exist as a fact only to their senses, not in the outside world. But it will bring them certainty that death is no longer a reality, for we can hardly entertain hope that anything slaughtered could survive" (B97, C25). We should also note how this example illustrates the second mode of existence, sensible existence, whose certitude results from the sensations which we experience. Moreover, it is worth noting that Ghazali selects this example, along with others which we shall see, from the quiver of sayings of the friends of the Prophet [ashab al-hadîth wa-ahl al-sunna], in sources noted by Jackson in his English translation of the text.

Such a choice emphasizes Ghazali's perspective: that of believers, to whom the five-fold strategy is addressed and who participate in a community whose tradition is rooted in the time and space of the Messenger and his friends, themselves the legacy – as he will later clarify – of the witness of earlier prophets who longer existed at the time of Muhammad.

As another example of this second mode of existence, Ghazali proposes a saying of the Prophet of Islam asserting: "paradise was shown to me on the face of this wall" (B97, C26). He then explains that Muhammad is speaking of an experience known to anyone, "of the heavens as seen in a small mirror." And he insists that anyone who might be distracted by the difference between a mirror and a wall will miss what is distinctive about that experience by which the Messenger was given to see paradise, an experience quite different from imagining it: "for you can tell the differ-ence between seeing the image of heaven in a mirror, and holding the image of heaven seen in the mirror in your imagination, after closing your eyes" (B97, C26).

For the third mode of existence, Ghazali proposes an example empha-sizing how this mode is rooted in the real. For as we have seen, images contained in our subjectivity presume the first mode of existence. Ghazali invites us to illustrate this mode "by what the Messenger – may God bless him – says: as if I were to see Yunus ibn Matta [Jonas, son of Matthew] wearing two wide-striped garments with short fringes, vowing his obedience to God" (B97, C26).

Ghazali reminds us that the meaning we give to this saying must jibe with the fact that Yunus ibn Matta was already dead at this time in the Messenger's life. So the Messenger was alerting us to the way in which an image known to those who had lived at the time of Yunus had become for him a witness to a living tradition. Far from expressing a hallucination of the Prophet or a resurrection of Yunus, this exclamation: "as if I had seen Yunus" rather testifies to how deeply Muhammad is rooted in the tradition. For

> this is obviously a reference to a matter unfolding within his imagi-nation, since the actual existence of this event preceded the existence of the Prophet – may God bless him, so was not in existence at the time of the Prophet's statement.
>
> (B97, C26)

For the last two modes of existence, the rational and analogical, the exam-ples underscore, the realism of the last ends, on the one hand, and their ultimate justification in the will of God, on the other. Ghazali is concerned to differentiate ephemeral and relative values associated with our present life from constant and absolute ones promised in the next world. Moreover, while suffering and joy are real rewards, justly willed by the Judge, there can be no hint of irascibility or emotion in the absolute constancy of His all-powerful will.

Proper use of the fourth mode of existence, rational existence, is exem-plified in the saying of the Prophet – may God bless him: "whoever exits the Hellfire will be given a portion of Paradise ten times the size of the world" (B97, C26). Again, no reason to be distracted by the plain anomaly of con-sidering a heavenly paradise to be ten times that of something worldly, for the bootless comparison means to express that the value of paradise infi-nitely exceeds anything at all. It may help to recall the terms merchants of precious stones will use to peddle their wares: "this precious stone is equal to this horse many times over" (B99, C27). The example Ghazali proposes for analogical existence is God's anger, taken in its essential sense of punitive intention, whose meaning was analyzed above (B100, C28).

In conclusion, the examples which Ghazali gives to illustrate the proper use of the fivefold strategy play a role identical to the role which the first mode of existence plays with regard to the others: to distinguish Islam from hypocrites. For like philosophers, hypocrites will have to acknowledge that there is no appreciable space between the two dimensions – objective and subjective – which characterize the world of believers. And if that is the case with them, it is only because they neither share in the meaning which most people attribute to existence, nor do they share in their hopes or fears.

Now we can consider Ghazali's examples of the way certain pretentious commentators will misuse the fourth and fifth modes of existence. Such misuse will display a profound similarity between certain Sufis and disciples of the *Batiniyya* on the one hand, and philosophers on the other. He devotes the ninth part of the *Decisive Criterion* (B104–7, C37–40) to those who "rush to figurative interpretations on the basis of speculative presumptions" (B107, 37) in an effort to expose their hypocrisy. His analysis here is the more significant in that the fidelity of these interpreters had not ordinarily been questioned, nor need their interpretations "be directed towards foundational elements of belief" (B107, C37).

This analysis, testifying as it does to virtues of finesse and spiritual discernment, will prove fundamental if Ghazali is to realize his project: to purify the believing community.

> For what lies hidden beneath the apparently innocent thesis of certain Sufis, that the meaning of the vision of the friend of God, Abraham – peace be upon him – of the star, and moon and the sun, with his words "this is my god", cannot be the plain one.
>
> (B107–8, C37; Qur'an 6:76)

These Sufis pretend that Abraham, the "friend of God," did not see the celestial bodies identified by everyone with common sense, but that he saw "luminous angelic substances, whose luminosity is rational rather than sensible, and characterized by ascending degrees of perfection" (B107–8, C37). So the "friend of God" would have discovered a world quite different from the one in which most of us live, a world resembling that proposed by certain disciples of the neo-Platonist school, who look upon sensible beings, like animals and plants and celestial bodies, as pale images of what truly exist, intelligible substances hierarchically arrayed. Sufis like these would persuade us that the meaning which most of us attribute to existence is simply erroneous. But worst of all, they trade on the excellence which all believers attribute to Abraham, as friend of God, to affirm this monstrosity. "In proof they insist that the friend of God – peace be upon him – is too exalted to have thought that a body, which he had just seen disappear below the horizon, could be a god" (B108, C37). Under the pretext of a philosophical theory of existence, these Sufis place in doubt the path traveled by most human beings, who are brought to identify the Eternal Unique Creator, by dint of the fact that everything around us is contingent and vanishing.

So the fact that the "friend of God" should have followed the same path is hardly astonishing, especially when we realize how young he was: "we are told," says Ghazali, "that he was a youth when all this took place, and there is nothing incredible about one destined to be a prophet entertaining a notion like this in his youth only to abandon it shortly thereafter" (B108, C38). Nor is it improbable that the heavenly bodies' very disappearance could be a sign of contingency for him more evident that any qualitative corporeal determination.

So the "friend of God" did not become a believer by virtue of speculation concerning luminous substances, nor by a perception according to which God would be perfectly intelligible. He became a believer by following the same path each of us has followed, who are called to become servants by drawing the conclusions to which we are led by the experience of total dependence on the will of God. So the teaching propagated by certain Sufis is truly pernicious, as they reject the conception of existence widely held by most people, and so threaten to alienate them from faith in the Creator and the path to the world to come.

Ghazali chooses the second example to illustrate the irresponsible perversity of the interpretation of certain "Batinites" concerning the adoration of the golden calf. Pretending that the golden calf passage cannot be comprehended in a literal sense, certain Batinites claim that most people would not have been able to consider what they "made . . . to be a god" (B109, C38–39). Ghazali shows that much as the presumption of Sufis led them to bar the way of faith to most human beings, in the name of an excellence they attribute to the friend of God, the "Batinities" bar the way in the name of the high opinion they profess to have of people in general. So he emphasizes "that it is not impossible for a group of people to come to adore [a crafted object] as attested by entire communities of idol worshippers. Nor can the fact that this would be exceptional assure us that it did to take place" (B109, C39). The crucial error of the "Batinites" lies in their inability to see how idolatry is rooted in failing to distinguish between all that is – plants and living animals, as well as wood, stone, and crafted things – and the all-powerful Creator of all.

It is hardly by chance that Ghazali continues by recalling those very principles of faith which it is strictly forbidden to interpret (B109, C39), for it is but a short way from presumption to unbelief; hence the need for the vigilant presence of a spiritual guide if the integrity of believers is to be protected. For he explains that believers are more threatened by certain Sufis and "Batinites" than by philosophers, whose pride leads them to insist that Revelation need only concern "others," that is, the mass of human beings, who only respect the law because of reward and punishment. Now philosophers who would insist that Revelation could hold no truth for them simply assure their legal condemnation, but those who offer to guide believers into rational and allegorical interpretation of the precious book are infinitely more harmful. For in fact, one need not proceed to interpret certain sayings of revelation whose imaginal and metaphorical character is clear. So faithful and intelligent believers are pressed – and should indeed be encouraged – not to take everything literally. For to abandon any critical sense comes to undermining common sense itself, as well as ill-serving the faith by inviting non-believers to identify the believing with the credulous. So all believers are welcome to undertake allegorical interpretation, just so long as they "observe the rules of figurative interpretation [al-ta'wīl]" (B101, C31). But such interpretation cannot be carried out effectively without the attentive surveillance of a spiritual master able to use reason without losing sight of the essential principles of faith.

Must we then conclude that Muslim philosophy is bereft of arguments? As we shall see in the next chapter, that is hardly the view of Avveroës, who is convinced of an intimate link between philosophy and revelation. Yet while it is precisely this link which will escape non-philosophers, nothing else can assure the unique status of the precious Book: a total coherence able to convince any reader.

Chapter 4

Averroës, philosopher-reader of the precious Book

Preamble

The two next chapters will be devoted to the original thought of Averroës, as an astute interpreter of the Qur'an by virtue of his philosophical acumen, as well as being able to bring Aristotle's philosophy to completion by virtue of the evidence his faith supplies for the existence of the Artisan of nature. The *Book of Decisive Discourse* which establishes the connection between revelation and philosophy is addressed to the political leaders of Andalusia, the Almohades, as well as all who wish to devote themselves to philosophical inquiry, with a view to elucidating the properly theological value of that inquiry. Contrary to Ghazali, Averroës is convinced that Qur'an verses cannot be adjudicated clearly without a rule of interpretation. For only those propositions are perspicuous which correspond with what is, yet it is philosophical method which directs our inquiry into beings, the method Aristotle provides to elucidate the warp and the woof of the all that is.

Taken in itself, however, this endeavor can only envisage the connection between philosophy and revelation from a philosophical perspective, due to insurmountable difficulties attending Qur'an interpretation without assistance from philosophers. So far as a theological perceptive on this connection, the Commentator's [Averroës'] originality will emerge from works he directs to philosophers, which we shall employ to evaluate the ways revealed truth helped him to reorganize the system of the Sage [Aristotle] (to whom sacred books were alien) in the light of the revelation of the existence of the Artisan – the subject of our fifth chapter.

A suggestive way to elucidate the actual rapport between revelation and philosophy, as an original and dynamic relation, would be a Moebius ring. The more penetrating is one's biological or physical research into natural things, the more skilled one becomes in affirming the beauty of the world as a perfectly ordered work of art, and so becomes able, in turn, to appreciate the utterly perspicuous coherence of the precious Book. By the same token, the more philosophers can appropriate the revealed truth of the unique existence of the Artisan, the more they will appreciate what remains to be clarified in the metaphysics of the sage Aristotle.

Finally, the more Averroës asserts his acumen as interpreter of the Qur'an by virtue of his philosophical skill; and as interpreter of Aristotle by virtue of his faith, the more he seems to deepen the gap separating him from the bulk of believers in the heart of the very community which he served so effectively in his long years in the role of supreme judge. This will be the subject of Chapter 6, showing the order we shall follow in reading the *Decisive Criterion*, whose first eighteen paragraphs will be studied in part one of this chapter. This exposition will be completed by examining the *Book of the Exposition of Methods of Proof*,[1] where Averroës expounds the connection between revelation and philosophy from the perspective of Plato, who affirms that while all human beings desire to know, it is rather those who find in themselves a higher intellectual capacity, philosophers, who will be able to fulfill this need. *Pari passu*, the obligation to engage in inquiry is incumbent on them. All this results from an explicit commandment of God in the Qur'an, addressed to those able to come to know Him by appreciating the unique, and indeed properly miraculous, status of the precious Book. This Book is able to convince all of its readers, despite radical differences in comprehension among them, while losing nothing of its perfect coherence.

Averroës will insist, contrary to Ghazali, that far from threatening the faith-identity of believing Muslims, philosophers alone will be able to secure that identity by safeguarding the unique status of the Qur'an as the anchor of authentic faith. For if all believers are equally convinced of the existence of the one God, it is not the case that all are equally able to appreciate God's transcendence nor the excellence of the world as a divine work of art. And if this is indeed the case, then Ghazali, not being a philosopher, could only deceive himself in accusing philosophers of unbelief. Averroës will devote paragraphs 19 to 48 to respond to Ghazali's accusations, the subject of the second part of this chapter. By daring to venture into the immense field of the precious Book, and arrogating to himself the right to judge and to condemn the first rank of believers, that is, philosophers, the spiritual master could only display a lack of understanding consonant with his degree of knowing. In examining the responses of Averroës, we shall supplement relevant paragraphs of the *Decisive discourse* by those taken from the *Incoherence of the Incoherence*,[2] as well as from the *Damima*, appended to Hourani's

English translation of the *Decisive discourse*.³ We shall consider paragraphs 49 to 72 of the *Decisive discourse* in the sixth chapter, showing the place Averroës will give to interpretation of Qur'anic verses by nonphilosophers, like Ghazali, as well as assess just how well-founded is the homage the judge-philosopher of Cordova pays to the Almohades, in concluding his work.

Part one – logico-philosophical inquiry into beings, and its theological significance

As "preeminent doctor of the law, judge, and a scholar of the highest rank by his knowledge,"⁴ Averroës counts on his double competence, as jurist and philosopher, to develop his argument that the Qur'an, as perspicuous word of the Artisan of the real, addressed to human beings able to hear it, cannot be understood without clarifying the rule of its interpretation. Furthermore, while this Word perfectly matches the contours of reality, it cannot be adequately understood except by those able to exercise the activity of reason to a higher degree than others, whose limitations keep them from carrying out rigorous inquiry. Yet for those able to do so, such inquiry is at the very heart of their religious obligations, stemming from an explicit command of God in the Qur'an. For such persons, philosophical inquiry becomes the method needed to elucidate the radical dependence of all that exists on the Artisan.

In this way Averroës develops an original perspective apparently far removed from that of Aristotle, for whom it belongs to natural beings to move themselves, while the "prime mover" or of the "thought which thinks itself" is characterized by an absolute autarchy rather than artisanal know-how. Moreover, Averroës opens the *Decisive discourse* by affirming the rapprochement at work between a philosophical perspective and that of theologians. For philosophers, in studying natural beings, cannot but conclude that it would be impossible for them to emanate from themselves, either in their constitution or in the coordination among them. Yet he makes this assertion with no claim to originality, simply proposing it as a matter of fact:

> if philosophical activity consists simply in rationally examining beings, and in reflecting on them as constituting proof for the existence of the Artisan, that is, as analogues of artifacts, for that alone would allow one to know the structure whereby beings would constitute proof for the existence of the Artisan; and knowledge of the Artisan is that much more perfect than knowledge of beings in their

structure, . . . then it is evident that the activity designated by the name [philosophy] is either obligatory or recommended by the revealed law.[5]

Yet if philosophical activity is an explicit obligation of the Qur'an, that could only be because of an analogy between the universe fashioned by God, the Artisan, and artifacts made by artisans. And if that be the case, it is because for those who truly comprehend, nature cannot be independent nor can God be the "prime mover" contemplating himself. In this way Averroës emphasizes his profound disagreement with Ghazali, for whom (as we have seen) earth, plants, and animals constitute objective reality as examples of the first mode of existence. Yet for Averroës, this first mode of existence, which may suggest the independence of natural things, merely testifies to the profound ignorance of the majority of human beings left to themselves. For left to themselves, without the assist of philosophy, human beings will fail to appreciate both the excellence of the structure – rocks, plants or animals, and the supreme know-how of the Artisan in placing them into the whole work of art which is the world. For though believers may be spared the consummate ignorance of those who imagine that plants and animals are simply there by chance, they still display a need for philosophy.

Averroës elucidates the differences among human beings regarding knowledge of the Artisan in his *Book of Exposition of Methods of Proof*, emphasizing how he distinguishes himself from Aristotle, for whom, "nature, in its first and fundamental sense, is the substance of beings who, in themselves and as such, have the principle of their own movement."[6] For Averroes, however, the more we know natural beings, the better we understand – by the perfect fit obtaining among the parts of these beings and the functioning whole of which they are a part – that they must themselves be the fruit of an intention, the product of an Artisan. In this way he clarifies two degrees of knowledge of the Artisan: the knowledge of the majority of human beings, and that of ones who know:

> the way the majority considers beings is like the way they consider artifacts whose construction they do not understand. All they know is that they are made, and that their maker exists. The way those who know [consider beings] is like a person who considers artifacts whose construction he knows, at least in part, and so can appreciate the wisdom it displays. There is little doubt that anyone who understands artifacts in this manner has a superior knowledge of their artisan.[7]

So those who know cannot doubt that animals and plants are not merely natural realities, but the products of an intention:

> the way [the artifact] proves [the existence of the artisan] is that the proof is in the artifact: by the order existing among its parts, that is, that some [of these parts] have been made with a view to others; and by the way the totality [of parts] fits the use envisaged [by the production of] this artifact, showing that it is not merely a product of nature but has rather been produced by an artisan who ordered each thing to its proper place. . . .[8]

It belongs to philosophy to try to comprehend the whole of scientific research, that relevant to plants and animals, as well as to physical science, what concerns the levels below the moon as well as those above it, and in this way attain an exemplary knowledge of the Artisan. This is the knowledge suggested by the verses of the Qur'an which Averroës cites, delineating the fit between heaven and earth, water and vegetation, which conditions the existence of camels. "Have they not scrutinized the kingdom of the heavens and the earth and all the things God has created" (7:185)? "Then will they not look well at the camel and the form with which it was created; at the heaven and how it was set on high" (88:17–18)?[9] For of what value is a perfectly adequate work of art like the camel without water and vegetation? Indeed, this question seems to underscore the inadequacy of Aristotle's position. For if every natural being is perfectly autonomous, with an internal principle of movement, how will they come to eat? And what rationale can we give for the ways species mutually interact?

Averroës then calls attention to the knowledge specific to philosophers in detailing the diverse ways of assessing the results of syllogistic inquiry. In presenting the result of inquiries, syllogisms adapt themselves equally to the range and the precision of respective inquiries, as well as to the aptitude of the pubic to be addressed. Given the fact that all human beings may desire to know, but not all are equally instructed or able to understand, or equipped with the same critical spirit, we must attend to the choice of syllogisms. Rather than satisfy the desire to know, an inappropriate syllogism will only elicit doubt and confusion. A good example is the knowledge which certain people have of the existence of the Artisan. A philosopher's knowledge embraces the entirety of beings in their reciprocal relations. It is as general as it is particular, and results in detailing everything human beings could know about the Artisan as principle of existence, along with the infinite richness of His intention, displayed in the beauty of the world. Addressing philosophers like himself, in admiration of the results of the inquiry by which they fulfill the explicit command of the Qur'an, he has recourse to a rational syllogism:

> since it has been established that revelation demands the examination of being by reason and reflection, as a matter of obligation; and that reflecting is nothing but inferring, eliciting the unknown from the known – which is the activity proper to syllogisms, or uses them to attain its goal – it follows that we have the obligation to have recourse to rational syllogisms to examine beings. . . .[10]

This kind of syllogism, called "demonstrative," is the most perfect.[11]

There are of course other syllogisms which others may use, as the one dear to scientists, more precise but less comprehensive, which would be limited to investigating a restricted field of beings. There are also dialectical syllogisms, whose premises are at best probable, so whose true conclusions, while generally accepted, are not based on rigorous proof. These syllogisms pertain to ethical and political discourses, which cannot be reserved to a minority but must be based on common sense and majority opinion. Finally, we have recourse to rhetorical syllogisms when addressing a crowd and calling attention to a particular feature. We must use them in such situations, for the public to which they are addressed is extremely limited in its range of knowledge, flighty, often impatient, and unable to tolerate doubts. We must note that what particularly recommends using the rhetorical syllogism is its capacity to convince without even suggesting contrary possibilities, though these may be just as probable as the conclusion the orator seeks to impose.[12] Hence the immense danger of using this type of syllogism irresponsibly, which can be the case with uncritical spiritual guides.

Averroës gives special attention to juridical syllogisms which conclude to laws, whose precise recommendations are similar to the rational syllogisms of philosophers[13] Yet for many reasons, juridical syllogisms are inferior to rational ones. Restricted to the practical order, they vary with circumstances of time and place.[14] Then they bear and mark opinions of judges and societal convention. Moreover, as the Qur'an explicitly mentions, they depend on particular cases. Now these particular cases can serve as a base from which they can be applied to other cases not specifically mentioned. Yet extending the properties of the paradigm case to a derived case only works because of a feature specific to the object in view, and since God has not deliberately indicated the status He accords to the case of beings and of things, we can only speculate what this feature would be in their case. Finally, like the rhetorical syllogism, the juridical syllogism proceeds from particular to particular, as examples do.[15] This last feature reminds us of the special use Ghazali make of syllogisms in *The Just Balance*, which we shall analyze in Chapter Six.[16] All of this indicates the deficiencies which lead Averroës to regard jurisprudence as inferior to a perspicuous science, even while emphasizing its obligatory character, which befits the role of judges in the community.

Let us now consider the properly miraculous character of the Precious book, and the way diverse syllogistic analyses can elucidate it. What makes the Word of God unique is its power to convince all readers. For the Qur'an, as Ghazali has emphasized, is the master, the unique guide, yet the secret of its excellence seems to have escaped the spiritual master, leading him to threaten the very cohesion of the Muslim community itself. That is because the truthfulness of the Qur'anic Word, in which all concur, assures at once the unity of the community of believers, as well as the radical diversity which obtains among human beings from the point of view of their degree of knowledge. So the Qur'an insures this diversified unity in calling human beings to come to know God while respecting their nature.

> for when it comes to the assent which people give, there is a clear gradation: certain people will acquiesce to the effect of demonstration, while others will give the same assent to the effect of dialectical argument, for their natures cannot dispose them any better; while still others will give rhetorical arguments the same assent which people of demonstration grant to demonstrative argument.[17]

The principle of diversified unity in the Muslim community displays a similar gradation, of which Ghazali can only show his ignorance, given that he is not a philosopher. Working as he does for the unification of believers, he was bound to end up leveling them, and by failing to respect the very nature of human beings he succeeded in closing off ways that might have led them to God.

> That is why the mission of the Prophet – peace be upon him – can claim this particular merit of having been addressed to all human beings, white or black, because the revelation he transmitted embraces the totality of methods by which one can be called to come to know God – may He be exalted.[18]

This unique capacity of the precious Book, to persuade all human beings, each in their own way, is intimately tied to its perfect coherence. For this reason, Ghazali threatens to undermine the very coherence of the Qur'anic word itself by insisting on the univocity of a literal sense, according to the first mode of existence evident to most human beings. Rather than being proud unbelievers, as Ghazali depicts them, betraying the limits of his own knowledge, philosophers are in fact unparalleled guardians of the unity of the community of believers by safeguarding the diversity of those who compose it. By placing the properly religious value of philosophical activity in doubt, and even worse by condemning it, Ghazali has attacked people whose excellence is perforce hidden from those who do not participate in the community of people of demonstration, outside the limits of time and space, devoted to investigating the unique Word.[19]

This community involves those for whom philosophical inquiry is a vital necessity: "to deny the study of philosophical works to those so endowed . . . is no less than denying a thirsty person a drink of fresh cold water, lest he die of thirst. . . ."[20] Using the excuse that someone might go astray or be misled by their study of philosophy, Ghazali betrays his ignorance of the radical differences among human beings from the perspective of their knowledge, so actively promotes a disastrous eventuality: a community of believers bereft of philosophers. Were that to eventuate, the very persons gifted with the criterion of interpretation of the precious Book, and so able to recognize its perspicuous coherence, would disappear.

In fact, the very meaning of *interpretation* eluded Ghazali when he distinguished five modes of existence along the lines of appearance, without supplying a fitting criterion between appearance and reality, thereby overlooking the truth of the matter. This criterion is found in logico-philosophical inquiry, the investigation of beings proper to philosophers.

> Now since this Revelation is the truth, and it invites us to practice rational examination which can assure knowledge of the truth, it follows that we Muslims know with a certain knowledge that the examination [of beings] by demonstration can in no way contradict the teachings of the revealed text, because truth cannot contradict truth, but accords with it and gives witness on its behalf.[21]

By denying the worth of philosophical inquiry in the name of common sense, Ghazali overlooks the fact that legions of convinced people can be deceived. Moreover, numerous allusions in the Qur'an to the paths by which human beings are called to God remain mysterious (16:125). The same is true of allusions to different gradations among believers (18:11), and especially verses intimating the rapport between knowledge and fear of God: "These are the ones whom God enlightens, those who have wisdom" (38:19). Anxious though he was to safeguard the equality of all Muslims endowed with common sense, Ghazali could hardly be unaware of the profound sense of these revealed verses, and so deny the pedagogical richness inherent in the Qur'an. Attentive as he was to the differences which obtain among those who realize their mortality and fear their end, he neglected significant differences among those addressees of the Qur'an endowed with reason. As for philosopher-interpreters of the Qur'an, he went so far as to undermine the very meaning of their inquiries, which in reality facilitate interpretation of the Qur'an. The section which follows is devoted to the intractable errors of Ghazali.

Part two – the coherent truthfulness of the Qur'an and the errors of Ghazali

How can we find our way in the boundless ocean of the Qur'an? How can we distinguish among proper meaning, image, symbol, or analogy; among affirmations, understatements, or recommendations, in this luxuriant and variegated tropical forest? In other words, how can we proceed to interpret without compass or plumb-line, the tools needed for interpreting? For

> what we do in interpreting is to move the meaning of a word from its proper sense to a figurative one, without distorting the way the Arabic language uses figurative language: anything can de designated by its analogue, its cause, its effect, its complement, or other recognized tropes.[22]

So how can we be certain that what may seem to be one of the figurative senses ought not be taken literally in the context peculiar to the Word of God? Alternatively, could it not be that what seems to be an ordinary, literal locution would, in another context, actually be a subtle analogy?

Averroës will proceed to answer this fundamental question with a confidence we can hardly share today, yet one reflecting his grasp of Aristotelian teaching. Here we can see "the manifest fruitfulness of the postulate according to which Aristotelian teaching offers the best expression of reality."[23] Even more clearly: as a program of scientific investigation, this method enables us to elucidate how the world is perfectly intelligible; yet the infinite richness of this intelligibility, as well as its import, will be hidden from those unable to recognize it as the consummate know-how of the Artisan.

As Averroës employs the acknowledged method of Aristotle to appreciate the excellence of the world as a work of art, he is also led to take the measure of the immense know-how of the precious Book. With his desire to know the world satisfied, and convinced of the utter truthfulness of the Qur'anic revelation, the philosopher had found his way.

> Given this juxtaposition . . ., two things follow. First, either the revealed text has nothing to say about the subject in question, or it makes a statement. If the first case, no contradiction is possible; in the second, here are two possible results: that the plain sense of the Qur'anic statement agrees with the results of demonstration, or they are contradictory. If they agree, nothing more need be said; if they contradict each other, we can always interpret the plain sense."[24]

So logico-philosophical truths become the plumb-line of interpretation, allowing people of demonstration to recognize the exceptional power of the Artisan. Equipped with this plumb-line, interpreters of the Qur'an can assess the linguistic richness of the Word.

> We can categorically insist that wherever a contradiction may arise between the results of demonstration and the plain sense of a revelational statement, that statement can be interpreted according to the rules of interpretation [in conformity with the usage] of the Arabic language.[25]

In response to Ghazali, however, Averroës contends that it will hardly suffice to know the Arabic language, nor to follow the sense which most people, especially those who are not philosophers, give to "existence" (that is, the first of the five modes enunciated by Ghazali); nor finally will it suffice to plumb their intentions, hopes and fears, either to appreciate the Artisan or fully appropriate their own conviction of the truthfulness of Revelation – "a proposition no Muslim would doubt or any believer hesitate to affirm, but how much more ample a certitude do those enjoy who are attached to this idea in such a way as to experience it."[26]

Equipped with this rule, philosophers can be among the first ranks of believers, taking the measure of the precious Book in its complete perspicuity and coherence.

> We can say even more: for any statement of Revelation whose plain sense contradicts the results of demonstration, an inductive search of the entire set of particular statements of the revealed text will turn up

another statement whose plain sense confirms the interpretation [given of the other], or comes close to doing so.[27]

So only philosophers are in a position to account for the quite singular characteristic of the Word of God whereby what appears to be the plain sense should probably be interpreted otherwise. By elucidating this feature they can appreciate the consummate fit between God's intention and the revealed text. For everyone to whom this Word is addressed, it is by virtue of this criss-cross of methods of affirmation – be they by images, plain senses, rigorous proofs, or examples – that God's will is realized in such a way that He is able to convince any reader. Hence the special duty of philosophers to keep their own interpretations to themselves. Otherwise, the very effort which confirms the way the Qur'an can convince philosophers could undermine the certitude enjoyed by others, by confiscating the precious Book for themselves.

So far from the proud cadre Ghazali presents, one sees philosophers as those believers called to the duty of vigilant silence, and so responsible for safeguarding the certitude which all share. For only philosophers can identify allusions in the text, quite hidden from others yet reserved by divine intention to people of deep learning, able to note contradictions between an apparently plain sense and a scientific result. "So when statements are found to be contradictory in their plain sense, that simply signals to [people of profound learning] that there is room for interpreting, in order to conciliate [the two]."[28] So people of profound learning have the duty not to divulge their learning, so as to avoid undermining the miraculous way the precious Book can convince any reader. In this way philosophers become servants of God and guardians of His intention, their duty being to keep to themselves the ultimate secret which is at the root of the evidence they themselves enjoy: their own conviction regarding the truth of the Qur'an.

Two possible interpretations of the seventh verse of the third sura validates a status peculiar to the philosopher-believer. As Averroës cites it,

> it is He who sent down upon you this Book. There are revelations within it which are quite categorical and explicit. These are the Book in its essential meaning and nature. Other verses employ metaphor and analogy, . . . but none know the interpretation except God and those who are well-grounded in the knowledge of it. They say: 'we have put our whole faith in it; it is all from the Lord.' It is only those endowed with real perception who take it to heart.
>
> (3:7)[29]

The reading he adopts clarifies the peculiar rapport which philosophers enjoy with God, in deciphering allusions buried in the text itself. This makes them believers *par excellence*, since they alone can appreciate the profound way that all that is depends upon the Artisan. An alternative reading of the verse differs from the first one given here by interposing a period to make two sentences, thus: "God alone it is who knows the interpretation of it. Those who are well-grounded in knowledge say: 'we have put our whole faith in it'." This reading indicates how, once philosophers have deciphered allusions to the divine intention hidden in the text, they will be that much better able to take the measure of the absolute transcendence of God, the creator, unique in His fully efficacious artisanal intention.[30]

Yet the duty of silence remains incumbent on philosophers at the heart of the community of believers. Far from being proud, philosophers keep the superiority of their knowledge well hidden, not out of humility but out of respect for the revealed text. Ghazali completely overlooked this duty of discretion as the lot of philosophers, with a total irresponsibility which led him to many troublesome misinterpretations.[31] But even worse, being profoundly deceived regarding himself and his limits, the spiritual master allowed himself to pass judgment on philosophers although their very discourse was quite opaque to him. In the *Decisive Discourse*, Averroës makes it clear that Ghazali had already condemned past philosophers, Avicenna and al-Farabi, as unbelievers, so distancing himself from the interpretation we have already proposed in Chapter Two, following Michael Marmura, that philosophers are not categorically condemned in the *Incoherence of Philosophy*.[32]

For Averroës, however, Ghazali had rendered a categorical condemnation in the *Incoherence*, though this condemnation was modified in the *Decisive Criterion*.[33] As the Andalusian judge specifies:

> Abu Hamid [al-Ghazali], in his work known under the title, *The Incoherence*, concluded categorically to their [al-Farabi and Avicenna's] unbelief with regard to three questions: the thesis of he pre-eternity of the world, that God – blessed be he – does not know particulars since He is above such things; and for his interpretations of revealed statements about the corporality of the resurrection and the modalities of a future life."[34]

Before expounding Averroës detailed responses in the *Decisive Discourse*, the *Book of Expositions of Methods and Proof*, and the *Damina*, let me clarify the more general reaction he expresses in the

Incoherence of the Incoherence. Barry Kogan has offered a magisterial analysis of this work, to which I am indebted in what follows,[35] though I must emphasize that I do not concur with his judgment that "the position of Ghazali is not simply anti-philosophical, as one can tell from his considerable esteem for logic . . . He only criticizes metaphysics."[36]

When Averroës engages in his refutation, in the *Incoherence of the Incoherence*, he is addressing the same public which Ghazali addressed: intelligent and critical believers who are not philosophers. He wants to explain to these people of dialectic and rhetoric that Ghazali offers no reasons to justify his aversion for philosophers, or the doubts he elicits regarding their enterprise. Directing his remarks to the more astute among them, Averroës would suggest that the vision of the world which the spiritual master, Ghazali, proposes in exchange for that of Aristotle, is actually extremely dangerous. Ghazali thinks he is emphasizing the lack of coherence in that vision of the world which he attributes to Avicenna – of its necessary descent from the First, the One – in the name of the freedom of its creator. But he seems suddenly to have forgotten the chasm separating God from the totality of creatures, natural agents as well as those endowed with will. In exchange for the vision of the world proposed by Aristotle, beginning with an ordered multiplicity which can lead us to conclude to the excellence of its Artisan, Ghazali proposes the vision of a world in submission to God's good will. A radical fragility lurks beneath the apparent order of the world, and beneath our moral distinctions: a set of beings whose laws give witness to what he calls the *habitus* of the Creator [*sunnah Allah*]. From doubting the value of the endeavor to search for causes of effects, Ghazali moves to denying that the search for rational justification has any sense at all. But the fact that one even may doubt everything does not imply, for Averroës, that one must suppress any difference between knowledge and ignorance, justified doubt and naive astonishment. That way leads to nullifying the very notion of doubt.

> Things whose causes escape us are in fact things which we do not know, so must investigate precisely because their causes have not been identified. . . . So it follows necessarily that things not known are these whose causes have not been identified.[37]

From this perspective the spiritual master is no more than an adroit sophist, rejecting what is clear and explicable to others under the pretext that there is no other way to safeguard the excellence of the Creator and his omnipotence. Astute masters among believers would doubtless be aware that Ghazali succeeded in erasing any difference proper to human beings endowed with intelligence – by which such people are distinguished from other creatures, though all remain subject to the confines of time; as well as bypassing what belongs properly to God the eternal existent. In selecting the term *habitus* to speak of God as the unique agent, Ghazali reveals a telling lack of understanding, for *habitus* [*sunnah Allah*] is a term linked with the actions of temporal beings, where repetition can develop vices as well as virtues: "a *habitus* which an agent acquires follows upon frequent repetition of actions."[38] In fact, Ghazali's very predilection for the literal sense of the Qur'an should have averted the danger he courts of leaving believers ignorant of the real transcendence of God: "you will never find any change in the way of God's will, you will never find any deviance in the way God disposes things" (35:41–42). This example should be enough to show the difference between "common sense" and the "literal sense," so as to highlight the disaster attending the Muslim community once philosophers would be estranged from it. For knowledge of the Arabic language, together with hope and fear in the face of the last things, can hardly justify condemning philosophers to unbelief, nor can these attitudes elucidate the rapport which obtains between the Artisan and that work of art which is the world.

After recalling the three theses which Ghazali pinned on philosophers (cited above), Averroës proceeds to underscore the inevitable errors arising from the way non-philosophers irresponsibly use concepts and distinctions which are quite beyond them.[39] He focuses first on God's knowledge, as presiding over the activity of creating as well as judging on the last day. Any discussion of this paradigmatically philosophical subject will presuppose distinguishing beings whose attributes change from the effects they produce in us, a point especially propitious for displaying Ghazali's philosophical incompetence.

Averroës emphasizes: "Abu Hamid misrepresents the peripatetic philosophers in attributing to them the thesis that God – may His names be exalted – cannot possibly know particulars. For their opinion is rather that He knows them by a knowledge generically different from ours. For our knowledge is caused by the object known, so that it is derived from the object and changeable like it; whereas God's knowledge – may He be praised – is quite the opposite, for it causes the object in its very being."[40]

By tracing Ghazali's error to its roots in a reading of Aristotle, Averroës can help us appreciate how his misunderstanding of the text in question reflects that of earlier commentators who also failed to realize that it is susceptible of variant interpretations. In fact, both Muslim philosophers, al-Farabi and Avicenna, failed to recognize the distance separating their path, which began with the immutable One to trace its gradual descent into

the many and all the way to a barely existent matter, from the diametrically opposite path of Aristotle, who began with a changing yet ordered
multiplicity to attain the principle of its intelligibility in the self-thinking
thought.

Yet for his part, Averroës fails to recognize the gap between his own
reading of Aristotle and the text itself. We have already noted how nature,
according to Aristotle, is what exists in itself and moves itself.[41] Though
perfectly intelligible, *nature* so conceived is the polar opposite of something produced and so existing only by virtue of an artisan whose intentions are completely comprehensible to the human beings in the midst of
it. Yet the Commentator [Averroës] fails to realize that evidence of a completely other order is required to bridge the gap between a self-thinking
thought and divine knowledge causative of being itself, without which his
interpretation can hardly claim to be perspicuously superior. Yet short of
this peculiar reading of Aristotle, neither al-Farabi nor Avicenna could
have been accused of the same error; that is, of failing to attend sufficiently to the multiple ways in which philosophical terms like "beings"
and "existence" can be used, they came to "assimilate things displaying
contrary essences and properties, which is the height of ignorance."[42]

Averroës finds this error the more regrettable in that it could have been
avoided by proper knowledge of the Arabic language, had they been
philosophers attentive to the way analogous discourse can discover similarities within differences, to mediate sameness and difference. Averroës
clarifies that only someone unaware of the preeminent role which
Aristotle gives to analogy would attribute to him the idea that God cannot
possibly know particulars – individual, animals, vegetables, minerals –
under the pretext that doing so would detract from His excellence:

> God is above all that.[43] For it is only by sheer ambiguity that the term
> 'knowledge' can be used of contingent and eternal knowledge; much
> like many terms which are used of contrary things, like *al-jalâl* [out-
> standing], which is used of eminent as well as trivial things. . . .[44]

Yet it should be clear that the gap separating God's knowledge from ours
could only escape someone who, like Ghazali, had failed to reflect sufficiently on the very notion of *truth*. For does not truth consist in a perfect fit
between what is and the definition formulated of the subject? Those who
seek definitions are people of knowledge devoted to investigating attributes with a view to grasping the essence of things. For even if every human
being is endowed with the ability to know, their shared essence will come
to light only by virtue of the differences among individual human beings.

For only by beginning with many attributes, linked with bodies which are born and die, can we come to know the essence expressed by the definition. Moreover, the definitions we come up with are not always appropriate, so our modes of knowing, together with the things on which they are based, are quite contingent, bearing the stamp of time.

So that truth which motivates our inquiry and is the ultimate object of our desire, will reflect the fullness which directs the everlasting course of time. But a perspicuous knowledge of God, as the principle of existence of those universals which are essences and species, as well as the individuals they comprise, together with their various attributes, will be something quite different. For only because God exists is there something rather than nothing, or can beings endowed with reason exist as well. So to speak of the knowledge we can have of God will require a complete mastery of our concepts of *universal*, *definition*, *truth*, and *time*. Hence it is hardly astonishing that Ghazali would err as he did, given that he is not a philosopher, though it remains regrettable that he failed so to recognize his limits. "So once we have shown demonstrably that this mode of knowing transcends the qualification of universal or of particular, the question whether to charge philosophers with unbelief becomes nugatory."[45] In the appendix (*Damina*), Averroës shows how this same "non-starter" besets Ghazali's way of safeguarding the temporal character of God's mode of knowing.[46]

As Ghazali sees it, given the mutability of things and their attributes according to the will of God; that is, according to His providence which is His *habitus*, God's knowledge of such things would run the risk of bearing the mark of their contingency. So he proposed that we distinguish events which happen to creatures; that is, changes which have their source in his *habitus*, from the immutable and perspicuous knowledge which is God's. In this way, he unfortunately displayed his profound ignorance of the subject of truth.

Ghazali suggests that such a perspicuous mode of knowing, while consisting of a rapport between knower and known, could nevertheless remain unchanged despite the changes which beset beings. What Averroës explains is that a thing known can certainly change without affecting the particular beings who are knowers, but not without changing the content of their knowledge, lest one lose sight of what truth means. It is not simply that proposing to distinguish the being of God from His knowing offends against God's unicity, but that doing so can only obscure what is proper to God as the unique principle on which all that is depends. And since nothing can change without first existing, nothing can exist without being known by a causative knowing.

Averroës moves on to the second of the three issues on which Ghazali bases his condemnation. Every bit as delicate as the first, this issue concerns the relation between the world and time. The Andalusian philosopher begins by calling attention to the bad faith which characterizes the very presentation of the issue, when Ghazali suggests that philosophers and theologians disagree significantly about it. As though philosophers who assert the "eternity" of the world *a parte ante* deny its total dependence on God; while theologians, in asserting the "novelty" of the world, were attesting to this dependence.[47] In fact, Averroës notes, they do not diverge at that point, which rather forms the basis of a profound agreement between philosophers and theologians – all equally convinced of the crucial distinction between the agent of all-that-is and the beings of which He is the principle. Leaving aside differences between people regarding the knowledge they have of the Artisan, Averroës emphasizes the fact that all concur in its existence: classical philosophers as well as Ash'arites agree on the fact that a Being exists who is not preceded by time, not of something or by something. "This is God – may He be exalted – the Agent of all, who makes all things to be and keeps them in being – may He be praised and His power exalted!"[48]

So this disagreement is not one between philosophers and theologians, but between philosophers; that is, those whose debates Ghazali would have characterized as "purely verbal." Averroës' contention here would seem to be ironic: "the discrepancy between Ash'arite theologians and classical philosophers on this point can be uniquely traced to differences in naming, especially for some of the philosophers in question."[49] Yet far from being "purely verbal," this philosophical debate is especially interesting, though it can only be explained properly in writings destined for philosophers, which we shall examine in the next chapter. In the context of the *Decisive Discourse*, Averroës had to remain on the level of images proper to people of rhetoric or dialectic, well this side of demonstration. Remaining at a level of similitude proper to Ghazali, however, we are reminded that Plato and his disciples were especially struck by the similarity between the whole which is the world and the parties which people it; that is, beings who are born and die. It was this similitude which brought them to justify the difference they had already noted between two vectors of time: infinite towards the future but having "a beginning in the past."[50] Aristotle and his disciples, on the other hand, were more sensitive to the infinite course of time, so were reticent about distinguishing between future and past. Plato would suggest we describe the world as "adventitious-eternal," while Aristotle was determined to call it "pre-eternal."

But call this can only be an approximation, which is all that can be offered at this level of image and similitude. In fact, the totality which is the world "is neither adventitious in the proper sense, nor pre-eternal in the proper sense, since the adventitious is necessarily corruptible, while the pre-eternal is uncaused."[51] In the end, however, despite the degree of knowledge of someone like Ghazali, we must emphasize the profound agreement uniting theologians and philosophers: their shrewd conviction regarding the radical dependence of the contingent whole, which is the universe, on the Being of God, so understood.

Averroës goes on to underscore that naming the world "adventitious" hardly squares with the literal sense of the Qur'anic word! To do so he will scrutinize the gap between common sense and the literal sense proper to revelation, thereby displaying Ghazali's incompetence when it comes to Qur'an interpretation, and finally, delineate philosophers' acumen in deciphering the plain sense, quite hidden to others. For if the only tools we have are the similarities and dissimilarities we can perceive between the Agent and the world, then we will be quite inept in accounting for the rapport between God, His Throne, the Heaven and change. Averroës then turns to verses of revelation, to show how their literal sense indicates ways of understanding time, being, and form and matter, which Muslim philosophers find in Aristotle.

> For if one undertakes an inductive examination of the Text, it appears ... that the form of the world is in effect adventitious, while being and time extend in two directions without end, since the divine statement 'it is He who created the heavens and the earth in six days – his throne is on the waters' (11:7) stipulates (in its plain sense) that there was something before this existence, [in this case designated as] – 'the throne' and 'the water.' ...[52]

For those first among believers who are philosophers, it will emerge that the definition of time is "the number of movement,"[53] that the form of existence properly belongs to the highest sphere, directing the movements which characterize our earth, yet finally to matter itself, as common to all composite things.

In this way we can understand that there are sayings in the text whose plain sense is reserved to philosophers as uniquely equipped with the concepts needed to identify it. Moreover, as we have already noted, philosophers are deputed to keep this interpretation for people of demonstration. Averroës then devotes the two subsequent paragraphs to recalling the duty of silence incumbent on philosophers, as well as the religious import of these discussions: that is, a propos the rapport between God and the world, and relevant to the competence of those able to recognize the theological import of existence. "One might well say, regarding those who find themselves trenchantly opposed on these issues, that whoever is right will be rewarded, and whoever is in error will be pardoned."[54]

The last subject motivating Ghazali to condemn philosophers was their treatment of the final end. We will recall that this subject is at the heart of the faith for him, the touchstone of the decisive distinction he proposes between Islam and hypocrites. Yet because this article of faith is so intimately linked to the other two, it becomes a paradigmatically philosophical issue, whose significance would escape non-philosophers. On the last day, judgment will consist in the perfectly just decree of the Being to whom all is transparent, the essence which belongs to human beings as able to know, with the varying degrees which attend them. So the just condemnation of certain people by the One whose knowledge is causative of being, for actions they commit according to a severely limited judgment, is indeed mysterious. Yet temporal beings of flesh and bone will be judged in such a way that their destiny will be everlasting. Moreover, our awareness that they will endure and of the time which will pass, becomes the very trauma of their lives. If it is hardly astonishing that all are convinced of the existence of beatitude and of torment in the world to come,[55] there remain anomalies which witness to the fact that human beings pertain to three degrees of knowledge, while the precious Book can convince everyone.[56]

Like the people of rhetoric and of dialectic, philosophers are intimately convinced that human beings cannot be limited to existence here below; yet they can be distinguished from the others in the meaning they attribute to this truth. For convinced as they are that immutable evidence can only be found in the realm of the spirit, it would be a betrayal for them to insist that joy and torment had to be sensual and their objects sensible – hence the demand for interpretation. Whereas for those persuaded that there is no existence beyond that available to common sense, proceeding to interpret would give evidence of unbelief or culpable innovation. Ghazali erred in bypassing these distinctions, in an effort to please everyone, yet in fact engendering doubt and confusion.

> It seems that this may even have been one of the goals of his books, and the proof that he intended this . . . can be found in the fact that he never followed in [his collected] works a single school, but was rather an Ash'arite with the Ash'arites, a Sufi with the Sufis, and a philosopher with the philosophers. . . .[57]

Averroës devoted several paragraphs of the *Book of The Exposition of Methods and of Proof*[58] to the utter perplexity which Ghazali's insistence on the explicitly corporeal promises of the afterlife caused among better instructed believes. He insisted on the fact that the afterlife is of the same kind as that here below, that it would enliven bodies similar to our own, though infinite in duration. Hence the insurmountable difficulty, or even the blatant absurdity, of trying to reconcile the irreconcilable: our perishable bodies with a life of boundless duration promised them on the other side. It would be the rare believer, who, endowed with common sense, could ignore that "our bodies here below are constituted from material elements participating in the formation of other terrestrial bodies, so could not exist at the same time in another world."[59] In fact, as Averroës explains, if there be an assertion which people convinced that the first mode of existence – of plants and animals – is primary could hardly ignore, it would be the incessant metabolism which sustains our terrestrial life. The remains of animals rot, to be transformed into soil which constitutes plants to nourish human beings who are born.[60]

Would it not better fit the conviction of everyone, given the very existence of the Artisan, to build on the Art which is His by suggesting that the bodies which will be ours in the afterlife will be of a kind fitting to an everlasting life?[61] Such a proposition has the advantage of saving the appearances, according to which the bodies which set us apart are in fact our mortal remains, whatever sense we may give to being alive. Could it not be that the causative knowledge of the Artisan would see to it that bodies of another kind would receive our soul?[62] Averroës speaks of bodies in the plural, and soul in the singular. While the analysis of his Commentary on Aristotle's *De Anima* exceeds the bounds of this work, it is quite significant that Alain de Libera's conclusions on this subject show how this grammatical decision perfectly matches his deepest thought.[63]

If that be the case, any distinction between particular human beings and their respective limits remain secondary. Spiritual capacities of the soul, on which philosophical activity confers all its richness, are alone significant. On the last Day each soul will be adjudicated uniquely, while the reward will give life to all. If this conviction were to have guided the activity of the Commentator, it would hardly be astonishing that he would link his certainty regarding the existence of the Artisan to his activity as a Muslim philosopher. That will be the subject of the next chapter.

Chapter 5

Reorganization of the world according to Aristotle in the light of Qur'anic revelation by Averroës

Preamble

Now the position which I have already outlined: that the Commentator was an original philosopher, in that the profound impetus of his thought proceeds from his faith, is hardly an accepted one. Hence my particular interest in other positions, like those of Jean Jolivet, Charles Touati, and Dominique Urvoy. All three of them insist on the difference between a metaphysics unaware of the creator, like that of Aristotle, and a metaphysics whose rationality stems from the certainty of the creator's existence, like that of Averroës.[1]

Yet in order to assess the ways in which Averroës' convictions as a believer lead him to diverge from Aristotle, we need to make the notion of *creator* more precise. According to the Andalusian philosopher, the Creator is the Artisan who fashions, models, composes and decomposes matter, rather than a magician who draws forth being from non-being. Given the perfect coherence of the universe, embracing as it does two domains as distinct as the sublunar one of generation and decay, and the eternally subsistent movements of the spheres above the moon, the inert matter and which animates the intention of the Artisan in fashioning it, need not be identical for each domain.

What is more, the new vision emerging from evidence of the existence of this wholly Other, the Artisan, demands that we elaborate the meaning proper to each use of this notion: that of the existence of the Artisan, of the matters which He fashions, and of the products of His artisanal art. The Artisan will be the One whose existence is identical with His creative intention, a perfectly coherent richness in no way limited by a specific essence, so quite different from the "first mover," act of pure thought, which many have thought the philosopher had simply adopted from Aristotle. And even if the products of the Artisan exist as specific objects moving themselves according go their respective essences, the matter which is found over against the Artisan has no motion of its own unless it be fashioned or composed. We would do well to recall the interpretation current in our time of questions Aristotle was thought to have left open, to allow the originality of the believing commentator, Averroës, to emerge. These questions focus on the roles played by notion of *substance*, Aristotle's paradigm for what exists, the notion of *prime matter*, and finally, that of the *prime mover*, or *thought thinking itself*, in the philosophy of Aristotle.

Despite the disagreements of D. W. Graham and of Louise Gill regarding the coherence of Aristotle's system, their agreement is singularly instructive for our endeavor.[2] For they are both convinced that Aristotle was a naturalist philosopher, focusing as he did on concrete beings for Graham,[3] or particular living things for Gill.[4] Neither finds the notion of *prime matter* coherent,[5] and they are each convinced that the notion of *prime mover* (admittedly coherent for Gill,[6] yet not so for Graham),[7] is utterly useless to account for the ordered changes which characterize the world.[8] Finally, the way their agreement seems to go to the very heart of their disagreement will help us propound the quite different position of Averroës. Graham is convinced that Aristotle's *Metaphysics* is subject to a radical incoherence which the philosopher overlooked.[9] To correct this oversight and preserve interest in the philosophy of Aristotle, he proposes that we renounce the existence of non-composite and non-concrete simples, namely, forms.[10] For her part, Gill is convinced that Aristotle's *Metaphysics* is utterly coherent so long as one renounces the effectively absurd notion of *prime matter*, which she proposes we replace with the "four elements," (earth, air, fire, and water), themselves composed of qualities which constitute them: cold, dry, hot, and moist.[11]

I must underscore the fact that both commentators are convinced that the very coherence of Aristotle's system demands that we abandon his metaphysical trajectory, which begins with many mutable concrete substance, only to culminate in satisfying that desire to know proper to human beings.[12] For Aristotle, by the end of this journey, philosophers will be able to imitate, if only partially, the philosophical divinity, the *self-thinking thought*, that perfect activity which eliminates any difference between the one who thinks and the real content of its perspicuous thought.[13] By emphasizing that the principle of explication of nature has two aspects, matter and form, relevant to descriptions of concrete things, Graham effectively truncates this trajectory.[14] More attentive to the foundation of ceaseless metabolism needed for the world of living things under the moon, Gill locates the principle of nature in sensible qualities, thereby renouncing the notion of *substance*, that is, the subject of qualities, whose definition constitutes the terminus of scientific inquiry. Yet if *fire* is constituted by the *hot* and the *dry*, what can account for the movement proper to it: "towards what is above?" What could offer a foundation rendering possible those distinctions presumed by the natural movement of the four elements? For the world of Aristotle is hardly one of open space, bereft of such distinctions.

As we shall see, Averroës' position is diametrically opposed to this interpretation. First, far from being a "naturalist," he sees Aristotle as the sage whose scientific method culminates in indicating all that one could hope to know about the Artisan of the world. Moreover, far from being absurd, the notion of *matter* is rather the axial subject allowing us to evaluate the import of the revelation of the existence of the Artisan, precisely to complete the *Metaphysics* of Aristotle, in such a way as to elucidate what is proper to the movement of composed substances, above or below the moon. Furthermore, without the realizing intention of the Artisan, that very coordination of movement to which our unique world gives witness, would be totally mysterious. So Averroës contends that the coherence of Aristotle's system depends on the notion of *matter*, as well as on the utterly unique existence of that One who is His own arstisanal intention. Hence the need to diversify the notion of *existence*: that proper to composed things in motion, that proper to their simple and intelligible principles, albeit inert before they will have been composed; and finally that existence enjoyed by the Artisan alone, whose transcendence only philosophers can appreciate.

Nothing displays the originality of the position Averroës takes in the face of interpretatons of Aristotle better than the phrase closing his commentary on book *lamda*: "nature resembles art."[15] This perspective assures the twin features characteristic of the commentary of Averroës: his scrupulous fidelity to the details of the Aristotelian text, as well as the profoundly novel way he reorganizes, in the light of his faith, their total context. This reorganization culminates in altering what Aristotle took to be the rapport between human beings and nature, as well as the relation obtaining between them and the *prime mover*, the *self-thinking thought*.

By introducing the analogy between nature and art, Aristotle intended to display what properly belongs to natural substances: to "move themselves" according to internal principles constituting their essences – what the definition signifies – which form the culmination of scientific inquiry according to the four causes (material, form, efficacious, and final). So the analogy between art and nature is conceived to emphasize what properly belongs to changing natural things: notably, the finality of each thing according to its species, for they are neither the result of pure chance nor of material necessity. This is the case because the natural changes which result, for the most part, clearly differ from those rare occurrences which happen from chance. Yet both natural individuals and products of art exist thanks to a form of a higher order which structures forms of a lower order, in bringing them to completion; that is to say, in composing a whole of its parts. Inferior forms, less well-ordered and partial, cannot account for the well-ordered superior forms, which constitute a functional whole, whether that be an animal or a house. The Greek philosopher never thought of an original artist, or of the Artisan who is impelled to "overcome" a resistant matter in the face of its resistance. Yet it is from within itself that this matter becomes the individual perfectly ordered according to its species. So art and nature resemble one another in their adaptability.

Aristotle has the art of masons in mind, by virtue of whose know-how what had been a pile of stone, of planks, and of iron bars, becomes, as if by itself, a perfectly livable house, much as substance moves itself, according to its form, that is, its essence. Unlike artisans who have to counter the resistance of matter, the essence of natural things does not throw up a screen to human knowers who study the orderly movements of substances to arrive at formal definitions. So the metaphor of art becomes fruitful for our inquiry into nature. Contrary to natural substances who move themselves, the *first mover* does not move itself, though it is consummately active. Its activity is that of thought thinking itself, which human beings can imitate on these rare occasions when they fully comprehend something, so identifying themselves with the intelligible content of their thoughts. Given that Nature functions of itself, the existence of a *Thought thinking itself* serves only to anchor the intelligibility of the world, so assuring that the properly human desire to know can be satisfied.

What can then be the status of matter, potentiality which is the condition of all movement but in itself resists definition? Aristotle maintains that philosophy can only gesture towards this radical ambiguity at the heart of his system, where it seems an abyss separates the limpid and unified stability of the knowledge of forms, of movement, and of marital beings. Furthermore, we have seen that in his vision the very fact of coordination among diverse species remains mysterious, though testifying to the unique order of the world, with the movement of spheres above the moon collaborating with the order of generation and decay below.

These lacunae and tensions could be resolved, however, were the First the Artisan whose causative intention comes to animate the matters which He fashions by composing and limiting them. His knowledge, itself radically inimitable, will assure that the movement of the whole, which is the natural world, will be perfectly coordinated. Yet nature would thereby lose its autonomy; it would no longer move itself, as Aristotle wished, but be moved by a causative intention, before which philosophers, become theologians, would be competent to take the measure of an utterly other, transcendent existence, that of the Artisan.

Yet this reorganization which Averroës works cannot be gratuitous, for it entails a consequence which threatens the very heart of the physics and metaphysics of Aristotle.[16] For if the ultimate principle of the natural world is the Artisan, unique by a now-how beyond our comprehension, nothing would stand in the way of beings emerging both according to enduring principles which are the species and also according to the infinite know-how of the artisanal intention over against the radical capacity of prime matter.

Hence the order we shall follow in the four following sections. The first will be devoted to the study of two kinds of matter, whose status was established by Averroës in his original work, *The Substance of the Celestial Spheres*, and in his commentary of book lamda of Aristotle's *Metaphysics*. In scrutinizing matter, Averroës was conscious of completing the thought of the sage by adding a new sense to the term "existence," quite different from that Aristotle had established, of composite substances in motion. The second section will focus on the cost of reorganizing Aristotle's system in the light of the certitude of faith in the existences of an Artisan. The third will show the benefit of the reorganization: to safeguard the transcendence of God by emphasizing that everything that exists is radically dependent on his intention. The final fourth section will resume the features specifying the position of this philosopher-believer Averroës.

Part one – two species of matter

Aristotle composed the treatise *On Substance and the Celestial Sphere* (*De substantia orbis*) in 1178, one year prior to the *Decisive Discourse*. So the lively memory which he would have had of a treatise in which he had expounded a vision of the world diametrically opposed to that of the Neoplatonic school could only reinforce his convictions concerning the proper rapport between philosophy and Revelation.[17] Quite contrary to the vision of the world established by Islamic Neoplatonic interpreters of Aristotle, who began with the One to follow the path of its emanation into the many, Averroës began with the many. Yet at the very foundation of this ordered multiple constituted by the four elements and their absolute movements – from the center toward higher and lower, and then all around – was prime matter. The four elements returned in the constitution of moving composite things, hierarchically ordered according to an increasing order of degrees of coherence and of the unification of their movements, up to the highest degree which is that of matter, receptacle of the form animating the imperturbable circular movement which describes the heavenly vault.

So prime matter, as well as the receptacle of the celestial sphere, become the two kinds of matter which Averroës wished to distinguish, yet without fragmenting the very meaning of matter or obfuscating significant distinctions between the two kinds. So he set himself to the task Aristotle had exemplified as proper to philosophers: to map the diverse uses of terms which convey the concepts needed to account for all that exists, doing so without falling into reductive univocity or equivocal confusion. At the beginning of the treatise Averroës reminds us that Aristotle had devoted many books to this subject so essential to realizing the human desire to know, and while regretting the fact that he had not had access to them all, went on to prepare his readers to identify his own contribution.[18] He then explains how the existence of two kinds of matter can be inferred from the way Aristotle examined the ordered set of changes which make up the world. Finally he makes clear that *change* is *movement*, the existence and meaning of which imply composition between the *moved*, which becomes the subject of movement by receiving it, and the one moving. So *movement* will imply composition of *form* with *matter*.[19]

From this perspective, beings above and below the moon share the fact that they are all composed, while principles of composition must be *simple*, or *specific*, yet themselves *inert*, whence derive the two kinds of *matter*, one as principle of composed moving things which decay while the other is principle of subsistent moving things. Yet a chasm separates the causes – matter and form – of transitory things from those of eternal things.[20] Yet since Averroës is intent on clarifying what is common to our unique world, the chasm will manifest itself, as we shall see, as a difference of degree in the matter involved, as well as the forms, more or less limited in their specificity. Our study of sublunar movement has already revealed this difference of degree, Averroës notes, since any movement exists in a subject and takes place between two contraries, identifiable as form and privation.

We should clarify how the subject envisaged here is a certain composite individual whose *form* is a specific attribution proper to it, while the *privation* – the absence of this very attribution – gives the change its direction. When a subject lacking a certain color acquires it, white becomes black; something lacking increases or diminishes, or what is below rises;

what was an embryo becomes a living being, while living beings decay. In this way, the privation which is principle of movement bears within itself a limitation marked by the category proper to it, thereby assuring the specificity of the change.

But what could serve as principle of all these limitations, the source of all distinctions? Whatever sense this question might have is no longer clear to us who are accustomed to the notion of empty and limitless space with no absolute sense of direction. But this shared presupposition is utterly essential to the world of Aristotle, necessitated as it is by natural movements whose absolute directions make for ordered changes. Averroës proposes the notion of *prime matter* precisely to account for changes proper to the sublunar world. As principle of limitation, matter itself must be unlimited. Subject of every privation, it is marked by the fact of being both "one in number" and specific, yet without possessing any distinction of its own. It is none of the four elements, nor any of the sensible qualities or the movements whose directions are absolute. For it is what permits all this, so this subject, "one in number is multiple in potency," is indeed an unlimited potency, as we recall.[21] From this perspective, the sublunar world is constituted by ordered yet limited movement, as we have noted, with an unlimited potentiality for enrichment, as is testified by the traces of movement the life proper to us.

Averroës turns once more to prime matter in his commentary on book lamda of Aristotle's *Metaphysics*. He emphasizes both what belongs to it as the ultimate subject of all decomposition and delimitation, on which the Artisan can work, as well as it the contribution it makes to that process. He insists that Aristotle never offered a complete clarification of the status of prime matter,[22] so making way for his own completion of what the Sage proposed, while remaining faithful to the literal sense of his proposals. Yet we must underscore how the more Averroës insists on features specific to substance, with the limitless privation which is prime matter, the more he distances himself from that world of individuals whose movements are entirely intelligible within the definitions of species. We shall return to this.

Averroës returns to the theme of prime matter by explicating how it is principle of the fact that the four elements are objects of sensation. Prime matter is the subject – one in number – common to air, fire, earth and water, while itself neither not nor cold, dry nor moist, thereby making possible the very existence of these manifolds, as well as the distinctions in their proper movements.[23] The Andalusian philosopher reminds us that *non-being* can be taken in three ways: the first being pure nothingness, which is not at all, nor can it be an object of thought; the second is the *nonbeing* associated with the privation of any form; while the third is that of potential existence not in act.[24]

We should note that, for Aristotle, the third sense belongs to composite existents as they realize the limited traces of the movements which characterize them, for composite particulars will never be fully themselves nor completely faithful to their definitions. So a particular human being, as we have seen, will only be able to "know" in the way that is common to all human beings with their specific limitations. Now the second way of taking nonbeing denotes *prime matter*, as the "privation of any form" signifies unlimited privation, a perfect "openness," at the heart of any set of dispositions and principle of the variety of possibilities. Such an unlimited richness is beyond our ability to think it, for it is principle of all our definitions, and the content of a primary intention. For from the unique perspective of a primary intention, the form presiding over the activity endemic to it is identical with the end, the goal of the object made.[25]

Now if the specificity of the primary intention – that of the Artisan, as we have seen – escapes us, that is because it lies beyond the limits of knowledge proper to us, even to philosophers, so *prime matter*, as the object that fashions this unique intention, will have to be deduced from the visibility of changeable things, thus becoming principle of any distinction. By executing this crucial contribution, Averroës succeeds in emphasizing what every human being, philosopher or not, knows: that visible variety testifies to the Artisan.[26]

This brings us to the chasm apparently separating what is transitory in the sublunar world from the persistence of the heavenly vault. As subject of the celestial spheres, the matter which receives perfectly circular motion is "one in number and in act."[27] Entirely subject to act by virtue of its perfect unicity, this matter will be at the very limit of a human knowledge whose forte is analysis.[28] Averroës emphasizes this difficulty in showing that the subject of a sphere is "matter" only in the sense that "matter" is equivocal. For while it is perfectly what it is, it cannot for all that ever be an object that one might fashion, define or trace. This peculiar subject is alien to attributes of quantity as well as to *whole* or *part*. It belongs to it to be specific, perfectly unified and precise, yet without being limited in any way. Indeed, this utterly singular specificity is "one of its virtues."[29]

Among the virtues of the Artisan is the way it testifies to the know-how governing the realization of the masterwork in motion, without our being able to describe either the subject of motion or its mover (which is the form) in terms of "parts." Moreover, this unique subject, as well as the form proper to it, are both simple existents, specific and inert before being composed, yet they are in fact composed. For the art of the Artisan governs the constitution of "moving things by way of the specific principle which animates it without itself being a part of it."[30] And the masterwork produced is "one, living, moving and desiring."[31] In concluding his exposition, Averroës is quite satisfied to have succeeded in elucidating the feature characteristic of a composite which owes its existence to Another.[32] Let me suggest that such an absurdity was inspired by Avicenna, for whom the "possible in itself" becomes "necessary" by virtue of the Other from which it proceeds.

In conclusion, reorganizing the whole of Aristotelian metaphysics in the light of the Artisan allows Averroës to emphasize what is lacking to a description – otherwise perfect in itself – of moving things, by offering an account of their existence. For from that perspective there is no difference at all between sublunar transitory composite things and persistent composite things above the moon. "Whether a body be generated or not, there is no difference with regard to its need for a force which acts, whether it be itself simple or composed of simples."[33] Averroës adds that he is convinced that this was in fact Aristotle's intention, citing a "force above the heavens and superior to them."[34]

We cannot overlook, however, the cost of this radical shift in perspective, for spontaneous generation now seems to be on a par with natural generation – a question we shall address in the next section.

Part two – becoming as the work of the artisan

The special attention and central place which Averroës devotes to Aristotle's remark regarding the modes of generation in book lamda of the *Metaphysics* testifies as much to the acumen of the commentator as it does to the awareness of the Muslim philosopher regarding the originality of the reorganization he proposes in the light of his faith in the existence of the Artisan. Aristotle says: "beings, in effect, emerge as from art, nature, fortune, or chance."[35]

His acumen as a commentator allows Averroës to recognize allusions in what the sage says to a lacuna which threatens the very coherence of the edifice of Aristotelian metaphysics, canceling any prospect that it had successfully demonstrated the possibility of establishing scientific ways of knowing, not supersensible ideas, but natural beings whose individual existence would reveal a universal essence. Such beings are accessible to an observation which, far from being the challenge to scientific knowledge that Plato thought, offers a way of recovering, in Aristotle's hands, the radical identity of sensible with intelligible. It is this identity which opens the way to the perspicuous definition from which perfect syllogisms begin: "I call that syllogism perfect which needs nothing more than what is proposed in the premises to reach a necessary conclusion in a perspicuous manner."[36]

It belongs to philosophers to propose the evident fruit of the activity proper to those who know, and thereby activate their ability to grasp the universal in the particular. This grasp embodies the intuition which crowns Aristotle's endeavor to show that knowledge is science, and that science is of the world in which we live. Yet if fortune, chance, and even spontaneity preside over the world of generation how can such knowledge prevail? What could possibly remain of the intelligible order which individuals manifest, and what might be the object of this intuition reconciling sensible with intelligible? We can, of course, find passages in Aristotle indicating how the sage does not claim certitude in such matter, but stays attentive to these so-called results of observation, emphasizing the gap between our knowledge and the richness of existence. For example, he notes that we are unable to demarcate the boundary separating living from inanimate with any clarity,[37] any more than we can that between animals and plants.[38] Yet this lack of clarity need not undermine the foundation of perfect order prevailing within the respective boundaries, as the movements characteristic of living things will testify. Yet his remarks about spontaneous generation of fish out of mud, slime, or clay – or even from themselves – threatens the foundation of his scientific enterprise.[39] For such remarks suggest the existence of cases in which scientific inquiry would have no object: that certain individuals result from themselves! Here one senses how the analogy Averroës introduces between nature and the Artisan offers immense help and incalculable advantage. For the analogy makes the natural order more supple without negating it, on condition, of course, that the primary intention of the Artisan will alone identify the coherence of his masterwork which is the world.

Yet in fact, the know-how of master builders allows them to reach their goal by paths they construct, or natural paths, or ones they simply come across. So rather than threaten their artistic skill, the presence of multiple ways and methods simply underscores their excellence at what they do. In a similar way, the unparalleled richness of artifacts, together with many ways they can be generated, will testify to the ultimate know-how of the Artisan. Yet the Aristotelian undertaking, which Averroës felt his reorganization – in the light of his faith in the existence of the Artisan – to have justified anew, now seems threatened in two ways. First, the identity of the form, as definition, proper to individuals according to their species, will have to accommodate an analogy of similarity, according to *priority* and *posteriority*. Second, there can be no more fixed boundaries between *constant, regular*, or *rare*. That is the price one must pay if natural beings, from works of art to products of spontaneous generation, are to have a place in a unique whole, notwithstanding their differences. Hence the importance Averroës gives to the subject of spontaneous generation in his commentary of book *lamda* of Aristotle's *Metaphysics*.[40] He insists that his explication of this phenomenon will clearly display how superior is his approach to that of pagan or Neoplatonic commentators of Aristotle, notably Alexander and Themistius.

So the philosopher Averroës displays his originality by the way his commentary safeguards the status of the Aristotelian principles of matter and form, yet by signaling their analogical significance, found antecedently in the highest degree in the intention of the Artisan confronting prime matter. He begins by noting how a study of the generation of moving things must proceed in the light of certain specific and enduring principles: matter and form.[41] He insists that this inquiry does not proceed by way of abstract concept, but concerns existing things, whose particular mode of existing often escaped commentators of Aristotle, who were all convinced that the only existing things were composites in motion.[42] Averroës counters that forms common to natural individuals, while certainly not generated, nonetheless are all *posterior*, depending on a primary intention at work as both form and end of existing things.[43] And we have already seen how this primary intention, from the perspective of its agency, unites into one its activity with the products emerging from it.[44]

So we can see how the existence of this primary intention both grounds the intelligibility of this unique world, and inspires scientific inquiry on the part of people of demonstration, yet does so by underscoring the limits of scientific endeavor by reason of the transcendent fullness of the primary intention. Averroës applauds the fitness of Alexander's commentary in elucidating the similarity which obtains between natural things and works of art. Nevertheless, Alexander misidentifies the principle of this similarity as an abstract concept, unrelated to reality, like that guiding those who would construct a mule out of "what ass and horse have in common."[45] Averroës locates the problem with this analysis in the way it emphasizes how natural things differ from works of art, rather than their similarity, however both may depend on artisans.[46] I would suggest that the Averroës' example of a mule fails by insinuating that works of art are inferior to natural things, by attending to the sterility of the mule. For even though a house does not generate itself, does not its very form make it superior to its materials, testifying to the versatility of its builders and the fruitfulness of their ideas? But Alexander's example leaves no room for the role of the Artisan *par excellence*, above everything else, whom Averroës has in mind. Yet we must note how this example is hardly foreign to Aristotle, for whom nature enjoys a spontaneity which rarely fails, yet avoids any abstract consideration.

Yet considering the dichotomy mentioned, Averroës insists that Alexander is in no position to account for the status of products of spontaneous generation, as they produce themselves out of decaying material, with no dependence at all on a "common concept," especially given their extraordinary variety, far more motley than that of natural individuals.[47] In the face of such abundance, Alexander had recourse to proposing, on the part of species, principles of natural generation; as the principle of artisanal generation, an abstract concept; and for spontaneous generation, a specific quality called "heat in act."[48] He offers no account of the status of *matter* as recipient of movement, and threatens as well the unicity of the sense of *form* as principle of motion, by parceling it out among subsistent qualities, natural species, and abstract concepts.

Averroës goes on to emphasize that this motley assortment of products of spontaneous generation had deeply impressed Themistius, who proposed that they could be the fruit of many active principles whose very activity would pass through matter.[49] Not without irony, Averroës suggests that we have here a commentator utterly unaware of that fact that he had "just rejected the vision of the sage. . . ."[50] Alternatively, Averroës underscores the fruitfulness of an originating primary intention, that of the Artisan whose existence assures that the contents of causative discourse be coherent. Yet the meaning of the term "intention" will be stretched to the limit, for the richness of this "intention" outreaches human understanding.[51]

Let us finally note how Averroës employs this phenomenon of spontaneous generation, which Aristotle would have been consoled to know was but an optical illusion, to help him identify the advantage accruing to the existence of a primary intention. For he proposes that the motley assortment of products of spontaneous generation emanates from a variety of "capacities and forms similar to the works of art" found in prime matter.[52] So such products will doubtless exist only for a time.[53]

In this way, if the "constancy" which characterizes natural generation, as well as the "regularity" belonging to works of art, can also accommodate the "rare" motley assortment from spontaneous generation, that will only be in virtue of the evidence Averroës has from faith in the existence of an utterly effective intention, that of the Artisan. Moreover, the coherence of a nature in which generation according to the forms of species can co-exist with the rare occurrence of things by way of spontaneous generation in Aristotle, that can only be because each of these productions take place of itself, whereas Averroës contends that nature owes its coherence to its radical dependence on the Artisan. It is only in the face of this creative intention, quite different from "thought thinking itself," which allows Averroës to sound the abyss separating the existence of the Artisan from that proper to composites as well as from their simple subsisting principles. That inquiry will be the subject of the next section, to show how Averroës can believe he completed the rational vision Aristotle had of the world, by virtue of his faith in the utterly other existence of the divine artisan.

Part three – the existent [al-qayyum] and the hidden [al-batin]

The crucial evidence of Aristotle leading to the fact that nature – the set of changing substance – is and explains itself takes account of the fact that, in studying it, the Greek philosopher had replaced the role of Artisan with that of the *prime mover*, whose activity is thinking. The prime mover serves to anchor motion and its activity consists in a perfect comprehension, to indicate that change is intelligible. Once a strict rapport has been established between being in motion and being intelligible, then the three features of reality – being, motion, intelligibility – will no longer do without saying, once they have been considered in the light of the analogy between nature and art. Neither change itself – sublunar generation and decay, and enduring circular motion above the moon – nor the fact of things' existing can go without saying any longer. What anchors change into a coherent whole, as we have seen, is a "primary intention" for whom to exist, to think, and to realize something are all one.

What all this elucidates philosophically is the radical dependence of things which move themselves on the Artisan. It is not simply that moving things, in moving themselves, do not do so from themselves but by virtue of the principles of matter and form; but also that these very principles are inert in so far as they are not objects of the intention which distinguishes in decomposing, and unifies in composing. Averroës notes that Avicenna completely overlooked this radical contingency of moving things.[54] Commenting on book Z of Aristotle's *Metaphysics*, he explains how individuals of each species are the form of the species to which they pertain. But this statement only makes sense on condition that a difference obtains between the essence, form, or definition of individuals, and their existence.[55] In fact, without *matter*, the object of the Artisan, there would neither be a visible multitude of mutable beings nor forms to preside over those changes. Finally, given that the ultimate principle of all that is, as well as its intelligibility, is no longer part of the world, it must be outside the world, and so *other*: other than whatever is in motion, as well as any limited or distinct meaning which might define it.

Wholly other, God, the Artisan, bears no resemblance to composites which change, whether they be in a place or be subsistent and distinct principle which effect the composition of changeable things, as well as their definitions. By contrast with composites in motion, God is what God is, in his simplicity; by contrast with inert principles, God is the Living One who brings life.

Given the way our thought and our language correlate with reality as we decipher it, Averroës emphasizes that God is absolutely transcendent. Thinking for us involves the ability to analyze, to which composites in motion correspond when they can be perfectly expressed in the criss-cross between subject and predicate, noun and verb, common and proper names. These grammatical distinctions reveal the deep structure of existence in such a way that we can understand that God, beyond all distinction, eludes both senses of "existence": that of a composite in motion as well as that of a simple principle resulting from analysis. God is the act of an existing essence in realizing it.

> In this way, one can comprehend what we have said of this one: that He is living and that life belongs to Him, must be a unique concept with regard to the subject; . . . the attribute is the subject of the attribute, I could say, since they refer to the same thing in act. . . .[56]

By His creative simplicity God eludes our knowing as well as the langue which expresses it.[57] Yet if God is principle of existence and of its intelligibility, could we not suggest that He is "the totality of forms in act?"[58] Is He not identical with existence? The response is doubly negative; first, since the meaning of such an affirmation would only be intelligible to God alone. For from our point of view, such a statement could only make sense as referring to a composite who acts or to "clear and distinct" ideas which are inert. In effect, the "totality of forms in act" can only mean to us something composed of essence which is this "totality forms," and the act which is its existence.

Moreover, were it possible for us to know the unique sense of the term "existence" as it is said of God, beginning with the use of the term with respect to the whole which is the world, there would be no difference between the existence of the Artisan and its nature. Yet while that affirmative statement eludes our understanding, it is nonetheless perfectly

intelligible and perspicuous from God's point of view, for His essence is
His causative activity, identical with His creative knowing.

> In truth, it is because He knows only Himself that He knows existents
> by the existence which is the cause of their existence; . . . the First –
> may He be praised – is the One who knows absolutely the nature of
> being as being, which is His essence.[59]

The terms "existent" and "knowing" are only said of god and of others in
an equivocal way.

> that is why the term 'to know' is said of His knowledge and of ours by
> homonymy. For His knowledge is the cause of being, and being is the
> cause of ours . . . the existence of the Existent who knows is neither
> characterized by our knowledge nor by our ignorance; and in this way
> [the One] whose existence is not other than His knowing becomes
> evident.[60]

So it is now clear that the terms "existent" and "knowing," as used in our
language, cannot describe Him at all, for they are not predicates for him;
they are rather His proper names, and philosophers know that. So the
excellence proper to Him is displayed in the fact that "people of demonstration" are particularly apt to recognize that the "how" of the Artisan's
existence is quite beyond them.

Let us also recall how the marvels of His work of art indicate to philosophers the limits of human know-how. Such is the way in which products
of spontaneous generation and those of natural generation find their
respective places in the criss-cross between rarity and constancy of sublunar time. Things are similar with the fixed stars and other marvels located
above the moon. These stars are "on" or "in" the celestial sphere, lacking
any "heaviness" to tarnish their transparency.[61] Here below, their light is
only called "hot" by pure equivocation with the light of the sun as it illuminates the totality of things subject to decay. The more the chasm separating the Artisan and His know-how from the world is cast in relief, the
more remarkable becomes the fact that He wills is work of art, without for-
getting that the term "will" can only be said of Him in a unique sense, by
which intention and realization are identical. And this is the case without
His being a magician or prestidigitator making something from nothing.

> That is why it is said that all proportions and all forms exist poten-
> tially in prime matter, and actually in the first mover, in a mode of

existence similar to the One who fabricates in act, in the spirit of the Artisan.[62]

God, the Artisan, wills [*yuridu*][63] His work, much like individual human beings that He has made from slime,[64] whose proper activity is to think, which only emphasizes the extraordinary ability of the Artisan. Averroës does all he can to distance individuals from God without attenuating the power of thought. He emphasizes the limits to the thought of human beings, who are only aware of themselves by virtue of conceiving another, and even this occurs but rarely.[65] Yet it remains true that in these rare moments human beings can taste a real beatitude, attuned to the fleeting resemblance between thinking human beings and the celestial sphere.[66] But is this thinking subject still an individual?

In conclusion, it should be clear that the originality of the Muslim philosopher Averroës lies in his beginning with Aristotle's paradigm of existents – composites in motion, subjects of scientific inquiry – and then knowing how to find a place for God. The creative thought of Allah, the Vivifying [*al-Muhyi*], the Creator [*al-Khaliq*], who knows every detail [*al-Muhsi*], becomes vitally necessary to the fact of significant existence in the world. Yet no one can speak of God except by selecting among His proper names. In the next part we shall show how Averroës made that selection.

Part four – Averroës, philosopher-believer

It would be difficult for us to imagine Averroës' deep satisfaction when he realized that he had been able to complete Aristotle's *Metaphysics* in the light of his faith in the existence of the Artisan. For we no longer share his justifiable admiration for Aristotle, the sage and author of what has been a unique way of organizing the whole of knowledge. Moreover, most of us would find quite alien to our sensibilities the conviction he had of belonging to a class of people for whom rational inquiry is an explicit commandment of Qur'anic revelation: "Say: 'Are they one and the same-those who know and those who think not'?" (39:12). Yet one weaned on a reverential fear of God, "the true architect of heaven and earth" (39:7), would find that commandment well-founded, and be inspired to elucidate as well as correct Aristotle's proposals. So it is predictable that Averroës would be taken by the names of God resonant of Aristotle's *Metaphysics* and especially apt to elucidate what characterizes our world of movement: Creator and Architect, as well as Living and Vivifying. In this way, the first article of Muslim faith – total and entire dependence of all that is on the one unique God – ever guided Averroës the commentator.

But what of the two other articles of faith relevant to our inquiry: the last judgment and the reality of the last end? I would suggest that Averroës' metaphysical choices underscore the very meaning that believing Muslims give to faith, quite contrary to a widespread suspicion regarding the authenticity of the faith of Averroës, "the rationalist."

Faith for Averroës is the acute awareness that human beings have of being arraigned before God. As each breath testifies to His existence, believers find themselves constantly before God – neither fearful nor trapped – giving thanks to Him for the work of art which is the world. For the world could not be any different or better than it is, nor is its beauty and perfectly ordered variety fragile in any way; none of our faults, inevitable consequences that they are of that lack of comprehension at the root of our distress, can affect it. For these faults, with the evils attending them, can but indicate the scope of our errors. The sense which Averroës gives to the term "good" as applied to the world, together with the sense he gives to the providence of God, as well as his vision of who we are as human beings – all testify to this dimension of his faith. The philosopher explains that human beings are less agents than they are acted upon and moved along, seldom acting on their own judgment, but rather moved by desires quite alien to reason. "The divers desirable things which move us are, in my opinion, quite alien to the intelligibles which move us. Since thee two motions are often contrary to each other; I would call the motion caused by desirable things contrary to that motion caused by intelligibles."[67]

From this perspective, Averroës does not seem to share Aristotle's view that human being are all motivated by the desire to know which anticipates that doubt and awe will be satisfied. He is rather closer to Plato, finding himself before a multitude with erroneous views, pulled apart by their passions "which distract us, and being opposed to each other, move us in contrary ways to opposite actions."[68] Plato finishes by emphasizing that human beings are so made that they cannot do what is good without adhering to "the collective law of the city."[69] Left to themselves, human beings can only call down catastrophe on themselves, and in their inability to understand that they are to blame, will look for scapegoats. "Rather than assume responsibility for their distress, they will attribute it to fortune, demons, or anything other than themselves!"[70]

Like Plato, Averroës is convinced that most human beings are quite ignorant of what they are doing, though (to temper the comparison) as a Muslim judge, he need not invent the laws because the best laws have been given in Qur'anic revelation, according to the primary intention of God Himself. So the suspicion of "Platonism" directed to Averroës is quite justified, so long as one limits it to Plato himself, and not to those who would style themselves his disciples, for Averroës has no truck with a theory of emanation of "the many from the One," nor does he share Plotinus' fascination with the *self.*

Averroës' vision of the world, as we have seen, begins with the unique Artisan whose intention is realized in composing and decomposing the two kinds of matter in a perfectly coherent whole of well-proportioned motion. So Plotinus' concern for the "self," whose "constant polishing" should concern all of us,[71] as well as the level on which one finds oneself,[72] is nothing but false décor for Averroës, if not the first step inclining towards renouncement *par excellence*: renouncement of the absolute transcendence of God to which Plotinus' desire to "flee, alone, to the Alone" inevitably leads.[73]

Yet the suspicion of "Platonism" would be justified if limited to two positions which Averroës shares with Plato himself. The first, at the heart of the principle of the analogy between nature and art, insists that sensible concrete things can neither exist by themselves nor explain themselves. The second – already mentioned in Chapter Two and to be treated in Chapter Six – insists on a categorical difference between human beings according to their degree of knowing. For Averroës, these differences are hardly the "pious lie" whose utility was promoted by Plato, but a reality imbedded in the excellence of the precious Book. Precisely because human beings are what they are, God is able to realize His noble intention to convince them all, only by employing the threefold method which correlates with their respective degrees of knowing. Averroës invokes the same perspective to envisage the infinite elevation of God, the Artisan, and so uphold his proposal for the proper use of the expressions: "goodness of the world" and "providence of God." This proposal has the special merit of being proposed as an internal correction of the image Aristotle offers to respond to the query concerning the relation between *good* and *nature.* Aristotle, in effect, puts the question to himself in these terms:

> In which of these two days does the nature of the whole possess the good and the sovereign good: as something separated, existing in itself and for itself? Or as the order of the whole? But could it not possess the good in both ways at once, like an army? For the good of the army lies in its order, yet the general commanding it is also its good, and even to a higher degree. For the general does not exist by virtue of the order, but the order exists by virtue of the general.[74]

In posing the question in this way, Aristotle has in fact highlighted the two questions which the *Metaphysics* had to leave open. The first asks how to explain the perfect coordination among individuals from diverse species; the second concerns the definition of *good* in his system. For given that *good* corresponds to the finality proper to each species, how can it also be what corresponds with the good of all of them? The image of the general of the army is offered to justify the good of each soldier as well as the good of all, suggesting Aristotle's singular view that army and general mutually depend on each other. But a chasm separates the general from the creative intention of the Artisan, as Averroës notes:

> the good which is found in the army's chief is far superior to the good in the order of the army, since that order exists because of the leader, . . . while the leader does not at all exist because of the order existing in the army, for the general of the army is the cause of the order; not the order the cause of the general.[75]

What makes the difference are the superior qualities belonging to the leader: he is he cause of the order of the whole without being included within it. If that be so, the leader is the Artisan whose intention is the cause of being *qua* being.

Yet we must note that once the good of the world is envisaged from the perspective of a creative intention, this question becomes properly theological. If the world is good, it is so because it corresponds to the intention of the Artisan, whose realization is also the most perfect possible. That brings us to the question of Providence and the worth of each of us to God. Recall that the Artisan cannot fashion individuals unless the form common to their proper species direct their matter. From this perspective, Averroës insists that "the opinion of those who think that the Providence of God attains to each person is just, . . . yet no one can be in a situation unique to themselves, but must be in one pertaining to their species."[76]

This is even more the case when it has to do with individuals able to appreciate how the multitude which composes the world coheres in a way which only the creative intention can explain: "what is common to all is that they exist because of one thing; and their actions all tend towards that One who is the first cause of the existence of the world." So the philosopher-believer Averroës can conclude: "the truth is that Providence exists, and whatever happens contrary to it is due to the necessity of matter rather than to the impotence of the Creator. . . ."[77] The Artisan, as we have already noted, is not a prestidigitator!

In conclusion, the faith of Averroës the philosopher is distinguished by celebrating the Will of God as he places himself before God. This posture of the philosopher-believer may also account for the profound respect he evoked in the Muslim mystic, Ibn al-Arabi, who realized as well how distant he was from so rationalist a philosopher.[78] The next chapter will be devoted to the place which Averroës found for himself as a philosopher-believer in Muslim society.

Chapter 6

Ghazali and Averroës in Muslim society

Preamble

Building on Chapters Three and Four, we shall now explore the debate between Ghazali and Averroës regarding Qur'an interpretation within their respective visions of society organized in the light of what is deemed essential to preserving the identity of believers.

For both protagonists are convinced that there is a way of assuring perspicuous interpretations of the Qur'an.[1] For Ghazali, this way is open to all Muslim believers, who can only be distinguished from one another by the purity of their intentions, which can never be assured. So he addresses the *Decisive Decree* to Muslims utterly equal in their status as believers, seeking to highlight two qualities – diagnostic aptitude and therapeutic art – which support his mission among them. One the other hand, Averroës judges that philosophers alone are endowed with a theory of interpreting the precious Book, itself a miracle of perspicuous propositions whose coherence will elude non-philosophers. So he addresses both Almohade leaders as well as a philosophically-endowed elite in his *Decisive Criterion*, to emphasize the theological value of inquiry carried out by "people of demonstration." So the Qur'an's miraculous power to convince everyone is nonetheless addressed to people who differ radically in their intellectual abilities. So in service of this miracle, Averroës has the duty to account for the role played by interpretations of the Qur'an available to non-philosophers addressed by spiritual masters aware of their own limits as well as those of their audience. Yet he is convinced that those limited in their degree of knowledge, and hence inferior to philosophers, will fail to understand these interpretations; which also means that he will be unable to justify the superiority of his interpretation of the Qur'an to such people, or show them how well-founded his conclusions are. Does this not spell a cognitive dissonance between philosopher and judge in Averroës himself, a tension which his access to Almohade power had effectively suppressed?

Finally, given that it will be impossible for him to make himself understood to non-philosophers, does not the responsibility for attenuating the danger to believers' identify devolve upon the powers responsible for public order? For they must attend to the danger that the public square could be taken over by debates on religious topics. Despite their basic disagreements, Ghazali and Averroës concur in identifying this threat, as well as in the steps to be taken to resolve it. It is rather that theologians, divided among themselves in the name of the truth which each one claims to possess, confuse believers.[2] So both protagonists would restrict or even proscribe such debates. For Ghazali, fascination with such theoretical debates could easily obscure the essential things which unite Muslims before the eternal; while Averroës cannot but commend those very powers who had come to acknowledge the theological impact of philosophical activity, so as to limit the influence of theologians sufficiently to allow him to offer sharp criticism of their ignorance. Hence the order within the two parts of this chapter, where each part will be devoted first to Ghazali and then to Averroës.

With regard to Ghazali, we shall focus on his radically egalitarian position, whereby Muslims can be distinguished only by their degree of intention, so by subtle differences which God alone is able to recognize or evaluate.[3] So the initial section of the first part of this chapter will delineate two qualities which support and ground Ghazali's aspiration to fulfill his mission as guide,[4] while in the second section of the same part Averroës will contend that the exalted opinion which Ghazali has of himself belies an ignorance of his own limits. Part two will focus on the philosopher's conviction that, quite apart from any categorical difference between human beings with respect to their knowledge, Ghazali has undermined the unique status of the Qur'an. The first section will examine the place Averroës reserves to non-philosophical interpretatons (like that of Ghazali) of the precious Book, whose miraculous feature is precisely to convince all its readers. Then from his role as philosopher-judge, we shall ask whether his homage to the Almohades concluding the *Decisive discourse* is well-founded.[5] In the second section of the second part, we shall ask whether there is any relation between the benefit of a power which "calls the mass of believers to knowledge of God by a middle way"[6] and the jurisprudence proposed and exercised by Averroës. Even more, does it properly belong to this judicial power to have facilitated the prolonged and beneficial exercise of Averroës twin functions of philosopher and judge?

Part one, section one – faith "of ordinary people is firmly anchored"[7]

The opening of the *Decisive Decree* is confirmed by Ghazali's theory of interpreting the Qur'an: the priority of the first mode of existence, as we have seen, as presupposed to the other four modes. Ghazali addresses, in the second person singular, a faithful believing friend, an ordinary person rightly alarmed by the uproar incited by masters of theological schools with their students, all of whom are at once naive and proud: "I felt you, my compassionate brother, to be in the throes of anxiety . . ." (B85, C11).[8] So he devotes the work to uprooting the causes of this anxiety. Indeed, the same error can be found to cause simple believers to suffer, once the unjustifiable requirements of theologians and judges have taken root in them. Failing to appreciate the worth of their faith, as exemplary as it is absolute, simple folk can let themselves be intimidated, while judges and theologians risk cutting down the tree which assures their livelihood.

Ghazali states that one need only read the Qur'an to grasp what is essential to the faith of simple believers, whereas confounding that faith is a trait shared by all unbelievers, imprisoned in their pride and manifold blindnesses. Explicit verses of the Qur'an expose profound similarities between the group of theologians, judges, and philosophers who make the audience of the *Decisive Decree* suffer, and those who resisted Muhammad by refusing his message. They share the pretension of possessing a valuable knowledge quite distinct from those accounts in which ordinary people, less well-endowed, find their fulfillment (B86–87, C12).[9] Ghazali goes on to explain to his faithful friend that he should never envy those persons who feel themselves sophisticated, especially on meeting students and professors of the *Nizamiyya* who pride themselves on adopting certain theological positions. To encourage the audience of the *Decree*, he assured them that as a faithful believer wanting to comprehend the essentials of the faith, he was clearly superior to all such ignorant imitators, quite unaware of the foundations of the theories they espoused (B87–88, C15–17). At the root of it all lie unconditional fanatics, along with masters of theology who imitate them, who have lost sight of what motivates the desire to know on the part of those to whom the *decree* is addressed, as well as of those essentials Ghazali had mentioned.

What are the neglected essentials? Each theological position is but a variant of that unique subject, constituting the principles of faith, whose truthfulness can be taken according to the first mode of existence that everyone understands. All the other modes make no sense if detached from the first (B96–100, C29–32). All theological interpretations are but dead branches outside of the essential, contained in three principles: resurrection of the body, paradise and hellfire, and the omniscience of God (B111, C43). And if the allusion to God's knowing seems to invoke learned distinctions between details which may change and essentials which perdure, what is essential to the life of believers rests on the very existence of the Prophet and the last end: "the bases of the faith are three; believe in God, in His messenger, and in the last Day" (B96–112, C43 [also 59–60]). In fact, the truthfulness of the sayings of the Prophet of Islam [ahadiths] lights the way of common people, much as the truth of the wholly other existence of God illuminates the inquiry of philosophers.

So the polemics of theologians (B101–103, C36), along with ideological debates between Sunnis and Shi'ites with regard to the imamate, all pale in the face of these fundamental truths. After his return from years of pilgrimage, though defender of the Abbaso-Seljuk polity, Ghazali has no interest for anything except what unites Muslims: "take no interest in people who exaggerate the importance of the imamate; . . . all that is excessive" (B107–111, C42). Nothing but the light of the essentials of faith will clarify what is essential to the life of believers. Ghazali recalls judges to what should guide their decrees and temper their condemnations: "the counsel is to avoid if at all possible saying anything evil about people who face Mecca so long as they attest that there is no God but Allah, and that Muhammad is His prophet" (B112, C41). One should take into account the essential note of belonging to the *Umma*: a visible gesture available to all human beings endowed with common sense.

Indeed, what could be the mission of judges so distant from the daily life of Muslims that they could no longer recognize those whose orthodoxy they are charged to protect? "If you come across a jurist, whose domain is exclusively that of jurisprudence, engaging in accusations of belief and unbelief, get away from him, pay him no attention with heart or word" (B120, C43). The sort of erudition which these jurists and theologians display remains irremediably external to what is essential. Locked within themselves, these learned men fail to realize that the powerful tool of reason is completely devalued in their hands. "Whoever thinks that faith comes by way of theology, abstract proofs, or ordered outlines, thereby commits an extreme heterodox innovation" (B122, C49). Indeed, for such as these, public uproar, disorder and violence may serve a salutary purpose, in drawing their attention to the real danger invited by their insouciance. It may be that an altogether earthly fear of losing their privileges might return these learned men to what is essential to believing Muslim faithful – simple people like those whom the Prophet himself addressed, no one of whom "undertook dogmatic theology or knew how to argue" (B124, C50).

Once restored to the essentials, Muslim theologians and judges will be able to recover their place among people, all equally distant from the ultimate perfection of the Prophet, yet each unique by virtue of the degree of purity and rectitude proper to them, whose exact worth is known only to God alone. Ghazali associates the multiple rewards and punishments of the last Day with this infinite medley, whose very diversity makes him use temporal distinctions to account for the afterlife: "Know that it might well be that you would be punished for a certain time and then released, or that someone whose sincerity in your regard is certain would intercede in your favor" (B129, C57). For the two poles of paradise and hellfire are separated by an infinite variability whose signification will nonetheless be evident for each one judged:

> there are those who will only be punished by inquiring into their actions, while others will come near to the fire only to be extracted from it by intercession, while yet others will enter the fire yet exit from it more or less quickly, according to whether their sins had to do with beliefs or heterodox innovations, and in accord with the number of their faults.
>
> (B127, C56)

God's mercy, which eludes our comprehension, manifests His unique ability, as infinitely just Judge, to recognize the precise worth of human intentions. For Ghazali reminds us that "this attribute of mercy does not vary according to our states; this world and the other only express the variation in our states" (B129, C56). Moreover, this completely other mercy also allows Ghazali to appreciate the absolute worth of Muslim faith. For one thing is certain: God's judgment in essentially tied to the real possibilities which human beings enjoyed on earth to recognize the Prophets and the truthfulness of his sayings. So for anyone who lived before the Prophet's birth, they are excusable. Others who may have heard his name were subject to the corrosive influence of those who spoke ill of him. "On the other hand, I insist that someone who has heard tell of the Prophet must entertain a desire to want to know the essential reality of this question . . .; were he not to test this impulse, . . . that would be unbelief" (B129, C56).

Finally, would there be any room to doubt the weight of Qur'anic revelation, and especially the centrality of final ends, in the face of the evidence Ghazali proposes?

Whoever has faith in God and believes in the last Day of all revealed religion cannot cease searching for the truth. . . . Should he undertake theoretical speculation and inquire without sparing any effort, yet death overtake him before consummating his quest, he will also be absolved and benefit from the vast mercy of God.

(B129, C56)

We must recognize that those benefiting from this mercy will not be persons content to know that each of these divine revelations is perspicuous. Ghazali has no time for people motivated by an ecumenical spirit as ample as it is pointless. He has in mind faithful persons of good faith, endowed with common sense, who have not spared any effort in their search for the unique and perfect truth, which fulfills and attains the entirety of Revelation. And should such a one die before completing his journey, his intention will intercede for him before God, because in his heart he is Muslim. So Ghazali is addressing Muslims in highlighting the two qualities which distinguish the vivifying knowledge of a true spiritual guide – the object of the following section.

Part one, section two – Ghazali: witness to diagnosis and healing

An authentic spiritual guide is blessed with an ingenious ability for discernment, which experience enhances even when he may lack self-knowledge. The decisive criterion for distinguishing Islam from *zandaqa* displays just such talent. For the Book seeks to respond to the urgent need to unmask unbelievers who conceal themselves at the very heart of the Muslim community, where they incite quarrels and so betray and pollute the essentials, that is the religious identity of Muslims. Addressing his audience, Ghazali outlines the path he proposes: one leading beyond what judges can say, with their knowledge of explicit Qur'anic passages regarding the status of unbelievers and the analogical rules enhancing their application. For juridical science only deals with the distinction between Muslims and those outside the Muslim community, the *Umma*. From the perspective of these judges, one might think that only the "others," strangers and foreigners, are unbelievers, and so liable to occupy that status which entails the death of the guilty and the sanction of hellfire. "So read the explicit texts regarding the status of Jews and Christians, deists, *zandaqa*, . . . while *a fortiori* the status of atheists is the same" (B92, C19). Yet notwithstanding the clarity of these rules, Ghazali notes, the essential prey "conceals itself beneath the surface" (B93, C20).

As we have seen in the third chapter, the proper use of the fivefold rule for interpreting the Qur'an demands discernment as well, especially that which identifies the manifest priority of the first mode of existence over all the others, as well as the absolute value attributed to fear of judgment. Without this diagnostic skill, no one could identify the feature common to all unbelievers who threaten Muslims by burrowing among them. For what could we find in common between philosophers, convinced that Revelation must be evaluated pragmatically since it only contains useful teachings (B110, C39), and Muslim theologians all too ready to interpret the perspicuous Word intellectually or allegorically (B107–109, C37), or between these two groups and certain Sufis especially devoted to spiritual exercises (B115, C43)?

None but a gifted and responsible spiritual master would know how to discern among those Muslims convinced they are better equipped and so more able to understand the Word of God than ordinary believers. So it is that all unbelievers concealed within the Muslim community think they know what is truly the case better than the audience of the *Decisive Decree*, or feel they have arrived to a state especially related to God, and so stand closer to the Creator than even his faithful friend. What a spiritual master can know does not result from special erudition or logic (B102, C35), nor from knowledge of Arabic language, nor even from critical expertise in analyzing traditions [*adadith*] and their authentic transmission (B114, C45). If all that were truly needed, entire volumes would not be able to contain this knowledge nor would any amount of time suffice to explicate it (B102, C41).

The simple truth is that what Ghazali has come to discern is hardly hidden from simple believers, the audience of the *Decree*, for if they were not endowed with the same gift, albeit secretly and without realizing it, they would not be able to follow his exposition. For the gift lies in recognizing what is essential to faith, yet it is only because the "brothers" whom the *Decree* addresses are already endowed with it that encountering it confounded will make them suffer, bruised in heart and mind (B85–86, C11). For Ghazali would be unable to heal these brothers were they not already faithful Muslims who read the Qur'an in the light of the first mode of existence, relying on fear and hope of the eternal. The spiritual master can bolster confidence in his friend only because they both share the same evidence that they may well be punished "for a certain time, and then released" (B129, C457). So those whom Ghazali addresses are inclined to follow him by recalling two truths. The first is evidence shared by all Muslims: that the Qur'anic Word alone adequately fulfills conditions for authentic transmission (B114, C45), while the second is the way the addressee of the *Decisive Criterion* suffers to see the truth confounded, showing that simple believers like them understand the revelation of God to his Messenger as perfectly as anyone can.

Yet if that be the case, how could philosophers be the most inclined to err, be those least endowed to understand the Word? That is Averroës' piercing question which will be addressed in the next part.

Part two, section one – the miracle of the precious Book with its diverse teachings

Averroës is convinced that despite his good intentions, Ghazali has moved well beyond explicit verses of the precious Book to undermine the astonishing concordance obtaining between the Word of God and philosophy, to effectively destroy the miracle of Qur'anic revelation. That very good intention moved the spiritual master to insist on a radical equality among believers before the Creator, but what could then remain of the miracle of a revelation which comes in a form perfectly adapted to convince each human being? For if everyone were equal in their ability to understand, it would take no genius to convince them all. But human beings are not all equal, as the Qur'an says explicitly. Emphasizing the higher degree of those who know, it says: "God will elevate to a higher state believers among you who have receive knowledge" (58:12); and detailing the value He gives to recognition: "Recognition is agreeable to His eyes" (39:9); while God Himself indicates the intimate link between faith and knowledge: "Those who have knowledge fear the Lord" (35:28).

Not being a philosopher, Ghazali could only remain deaf to the astonishing harmony between these references and the teaching of Plato and Aristotle. Plato had clearly indicated how human beings are fundamentally distinguished from one another by their respective degrees of knowledge, as Aristotle detailed how syllogisms are ordered hierarchically in their capacity to convince.[10] By dispensing with radical differences among believers, and putting himself in the place of philosophers to propose a theory of interpreting the Book, Ghazali displayed a profound ignorance of the miracle of Revelation: its ability to convince all human beings according to their respective degrees of knowledge, and to do so without disturbing its perfect coherence.[11] God speaks the unique truth in multiple ways to lead everyone to that "happiness which is knowledge of God."[12]

By applying to revelation the metaphysical skills associated with Aristotle – distinguishing without fracturing, Averroës emphasizes that revelation is not simply a matter of polyvalent expressions, but of chains of syllogistic proofs designed to illuminate a unique truth fitted to convincing human beings diversely endowed with critical spirit.[13] In this way, the Qur'an, as perspicuous Word of the Creator addressed to beings diversely endowed with reason, becomes the pedagogical paradigm introducing believers to the order proper to a heterogeneous society, alone able to conserve significant differences without undermining the unity of believers.

Within such a well-ordered society, one will be able to recognize what is common to all human beings as well as what distinguishes some from others. What they share in common is their ability to be astonished, whereas the ability of each to be satisfied by the explanations offered will distinguish one from the other. From this perspective, the concordance between the literal sense of Qur'anic verses and the statements of philosophers plays a special role, since it indicates an astonishing fact which all can appreciate. Yet this evident concordance differs from the reciprocal connection between philosophy and revelation analyzed in Chapters Four and Five. Both dimensions of this connection emphasize the excellence of philosophy, whether it be in interpreting the Book (Chapter Four) or in the ability to find in revelation light needed to complete Aristotle's *Metaphysics* (Chapter Five). But the fact of a line of concordance is evident to any reader of the Qur'an inclined to read the classical philosophers, even to take issue with them.

From his good intentions, Ghazali had erased any difference between human beings from the point of view of their knowledge, only to end up neglecting the precise feature which could have connected all Muslims endowed with a common sense capable of astonishment. In emphasizing this point of contact, Averroës suggests that the issue of rapport between philosophy and revelation is rooted in the astonishment evinced by reflective readers of the Qur'an. In the light of this feature which all believers share, philosophers – alone able to appreciate the perspicuous coherence of the precious Book while respecting the duty of silence which their degree of knowledge imposes on them – will nonetheless be able to counsel others, especially spiritual masters. They can do so by teaching them how to guide others who are not philosophers in their reading of the Qur'an, while respecting their own limits. Averroës chooses as his examples the Qur'an verse which evokes God's being seated on His Throne as well as the tradition [*hadith*] which describes God's descent from it.[14]

This verse is particularly salient in that Ghazali used it to introduce subjects which must be understood according to the first mode of existence, that is, literally with no need for interpretation: "The all-Merciful is seated in majesty on the Throne" (20:5). Contrary to Ghazali, Averroës

emphasizes how a verse like this must forcibly awaken in believers a justified astonishment, so it would be wrong not to guide them in their desire
to understand what significance it might convey for the existence of God.

Reminding ourselves that Ghazali left no place for philosophers among
believers, it is noteworthy that while possessed of the conviction that he
alone can understand the real transcendence of the existence of God,
Averroës finds himself interested in the efforts of non-philosophers to
approach the meaning of the existence of God. This openness leads him to
emphasize the feature of Qur'anic revelation which, contrary to Ghazali,
never decrees whether the attribute of corporality ought or ought not to be
attributed to God. More precisely:

> I would assert that it is obligatory regarding this attribute, to follow
> the path delineated in revelation, so to forbear pronouncing positively
> or negatively . . . The crowd takes being to be imaginable or sensible,
> and what cannot be imagined or sensed does not exist. So that if one
> were to say that there is a being who is not bodily, we would eliminate
> the possibility of imagining it, so this being would be relegated by
> them to the order of non-existence.[15]

Averroës goes on to note that even some for whom a being need not be
sensible or imaginable might well think that no being could be without a
place. For that reason, he insists, "we must respond . . . that this has to do
with 'equivocal verses'."[16] One should also note that these verses in particular become objects of divergence even among "people of demonstration," who are that much better endowed to understand.

Yet other verses of revelation are better adapted to the use which a spiritual master might make of them, aware of his limits and devoted to the
direction of believers. Averroës takes them into consideration in the pages
devoted to allegorical interpretation.[17] Noting how these concern texts
which evoke symbolic meaning, he proposes dividing them into four categories, according to the measure of doubt as well as the identification of
symbolic language with regard to its meaning. These two criteria are intimately linked to the exceptional status of the Book, whose coherence will
escape non-philosophers, unable as they are to identify allusions hidden in
Revelation for the attention of "people of demonstration." Indeed, certain
verses are expressed so that their plain sense apparently contradicts what
"people of profound knowledge" alone know to be demonstrated truth,
though this contradiction will be hidden from others.[18]

So there may be texts whose language, while apparently literal, should
not be read like others where the symbolic language is rather a screen to be

surmounted. Yet if this be the case, then far from convincing everyone of the unique truth, the precious Book hides it from most of them. Can the Qur'an be so enigmatic, be a criss-cross so wisely organized as to safe-guard a secret of which most believers will be unaware, including that of existence itself? But such texts do exist, Averroës insists, grouping them into four categories. The first is entitled: "where it is difficult to recognize whether it is a matter of symbolism,[19] and in what sense." The fourth is entitled: "where it is difficult to recognize the existence of symbols but easy to recognize their meaning."[20] These two categories include texts whose interpretation is reserved to "those who know."

There are still other texts, collected under the second and third cate-gories, which form a bridge between the mass of believers and revelation by sustaining a life shared.[21] The second category groups texts whose symbolic language renders meanings easily recognizable, so everyone is invited to take part in their interpretatons. Regrettably, Averroës fails to propose examples of these texts which sustain the prayer life everyone shares – rhetorical sentences, allegorical poems, and parables. Indeed, to fail to recognize their symbolic language, or ask what they might mean, could only signal one's alienation from the community. In this way, mas-tery of a certain poetic genre gives evidence to everyone of membership in the community, in such a way that no one could question it except strangers to whom the language is alien.

Finally the third category contains texts whose allegorical language is easy to recognize but whose meaning remains enigmatic.[22] Think of the Prophet's saying: "the black stone is the right hand of God on earth." Recall that Ghazali cited this text to show how everyone, including tradi-tionalists like Ibn Hanbal, are compelled to engage in allegorical interpre-tation. Once he had indicated Ghazali's fundamental error, of reserving the right to interpret everything in revelation, and specifically what is essential to it – fundamental articles like the sensible nature of punishment and rewards in after life, Averroës will insist on employing texts assem-bled under the third category to test Ghazali's theories. For given their enigmatic character, and their evidently symbolic language, he shows how only those who pertain to a certain elite – even if they are not "people of demonstration" – can be trusted to interpret them. Moreover, these texts are the very ones which believers ought to be able to understand with the help of Ghazali's fivefold rule of interpretation. Not without irony, he goes on to explicate that the very ones to whom Ghazali ought to have directed his teaching are those able to apprehend "that one and the same thing can have five modes of existence!"[23] For such persons, there could be no fault in choosing the mode which fit them best. Averroës proposes other examples concerning paradise, hellfire, and even eternal life. "Dust consumes all of a son of Adam except his coccyx."[24]

Given the import Ghazali gives to texts concerning fear and hope for the final end, we should note the chasm separating the two protagonists. For Averroës, such texts are clearly symbolic. Manifestly enigmatic, they give rise to questions from everyone, so a responsible spiritual master, aware of his limits, should be able to recognize those whose doubts and anxieties would be met through an interpretation effecting harmony among the five modes of existence. Pinpointing Ghazali's major fault, as well as his inability to correct it, Averroës concludes by noting that "Abu Hamid made no such distinction."[25] Unaware of his own limits, Ghazali has "sinned against revelation and philosophy, even if he believed he had done well."[26]

But what can philosophy expect to do, held back by the duty of silence which its degree of knowledge imposes, as well as by the incapacity of others, limited in their own ways? Averroës turned to political leaders of the community to remind them of their duty to preserve order.[27] For the Almohades, the "conquering power,"[28] whom he had long served in the dual role of judge and philosopher, had been able to work judiciously towards a well-ordered society of believer. This was due primarily to Abu Yacub Yussuf, a privileged reader of the *Decisive discourse*, whom Averroës praises at the end of this work. What could have motivated such an eulogy, or justified the gratitude which the philosopher-judge Averroës felt the need to express? We shall consider that next.

Part two, section two – the philosopher-judge, "a striver [al-mujtihad]" in interpreting the Qur'an and his homage to the Almohades

We need to be grateful to Roger Arnaldez for showing how the role of judge affects the thought and the person of Averroës.[29] Indeed, that very clarification makes us regret the more his silence about certain interferences, sources of tension, ever mollified, thanks to the clear and pragmatic balance of Almohade power, which motivated the eulogy appended to the end of the *Decisive discourse*. This homage to the conquering power manifests Averroës' confidence in the politico-religious reform by which he had been able to overcome these tensions.

> God has put an end to many . . . of these pernicious tendencies, thanks to the conquering power. By them He opened the way to numerous

benefits, especially for that class of persons engaged in the path of rational inquiry, aspiring to know the truth. They called the mass of people to the knowledge of God – may He be praised – by a middle way beyond the low level of imitative conformism, yet below the pointless debates of dialectical theologians; as he showed the elite the necessity of engaging radically in rational inquiry into the source of revelation.[30]

The primary benefit of this power was its way of recognizing the properly theological value of philosophical activity among "people of demonstration," giving it priority over that of theologians. Averroës shares Ghazali's judgment regarding these self-proclaimed leaders of Islamic sects "who have come to the point of accusing one another of unbelief or blameworthy innovation . . .,"[31] even as they are themselves ignorant of the condition of validity of proofs as well as the intellectual capacity of their public. "The methods they use to establish [the validity of] their interpretation fit neither the crowd nor the elite, for on examining them one realizes that they do not satisfy conditions of demonstration."[32] In this way, these "speculative thinkers who have become oppressors of Muslims"[33] have failed to usurp the place of philosophers as interpreters of revelation, who are alone able to recognize its absolutely perspicuous coherence, while respecting diverse intellectual abilities of believers. In the absence of his political power, such theologians would be likely to corrupt revelation itself as well as turn people away from it.[34] Upon completing the *Decisive discourse*, which accounted for the linkage between revelation and philosophy from a philosophical perspective, with the substance of the celestial sphere illuminating the same connection from the perspective of Revelation with the existence of the Artisan, Averroës praised the one who would have appreciated his dual achievement, Abu Yacub Yussuf, for having recognized the theological worth of philosophers who undertook the path of rational inquiry and aspired to know the truth.[35]

The second benefit of this power lies in the way it called the community to knowledge of God by a "middle way," founded on the jurisprudence executed by Averroës, the judge who based his decrees on these "principles," that is verses of the Qur'an. This path is beyond the imitative conformism of the Malikites, who were satisfied to follow the precedents of the traditions of Medina, the city of the Prophet. A profoundly pragmatic know-how was needed to give a place to judges who would "force themselves" to deduce from verses of the Qur'an what would allow them to guide the daily lives of believers, without attending to what they may have thought of the Maliki tradition.[36] Like his grandfather, Averroës belonged to this tradition, and in doing so opened a revolution admitting that a responsible judge could interpret the Qur'an in the light of reason and not simply from precedent.[37]

Beyond the "low level of conformism," the middle way by which the people are called to God is situated "below the eristic of dialectical theologians."[38] It is certainly located below that of "people of demonstration," but who would these dialectical theologians be? Would they be theologians ignorant of the conditions of proof we have seen? Probably not, for any method works for charlatans. Furthermore, by an irony close to pure sarcasm, these "speculative thinkers who have become oppressors of Muslims"[39] are in no way "above" any path whatsoever. I would suggest that these dialecticians are theologians who try to defend the very principles of the founder of the Almohades the Mahdi Ibn Tumart, who demanded that everyone, without distinguishing crowd from elite, recognize the transcendent existence of God.[40]

The third motive for eulogizing the conquering power could be that he understood that to try to demand the impossible, that is, that everyone would be able to preserve their faith in God by accepting his total otherness, would risk their losing hold of the certitude of his existence. So we might suppose that Averroës thought the Almohade, Abu Yacub Yussuf, shared his conviction that it would be preferable to follow Qur'anic revelation, and "not pronounce, either positively or negatively," on the attribute of corporality of God.[41] To demand that everyone become philosophers would amount to pretending to change human nature itself, so on the basis of a utopian intention, could end up diverting human beings from the essential which is certitude of the existence of God. So the third motive for this eulogy of power would be Averroës' profound respect for those able to adjust their demands so as to preserve what is essential to the existence of a community of believers.[42]

So Averroës praises the realistic and enlightened pragmatism of the Almohades to have worked out a way of confirming a community of believers while respecting the diversity of intellectual abilities of the people who compose it, by acknowledging the elite as well as calling the crowd to knowledge of God by a middle way. That would then be the way of juridical syllogism, located below the demonstrative syllogism of philosophy. Failing to do the impossible, we should recall, hardly testifies to the inadequacy of artisans, including those crafting the political order, but rather shows how matter can limit the undertakings of human beings with diverse abilities to understand.

Finally, there is the last motive for this eulogy given to power: that he had facilitated Averroës' long and fruitful activity as both philosopher and supreme judge. He was a judge who "forced himself" neither to succumb to nor to reject the fact that he belonged to the Maliki tradition, nor to overlook the duty of silence which his excellence as a philosopher imposed on him, as alone able to interpret fully revelation. Roger Arnaldez explains the judge is not obliged to convince those whom he judges.[43] Yet must he not account for his judgments to his peers, other judges and especially Maliki judges whom he considered to be inferior? I would suggest that the duty of silence, observed by this judge in the name of the excellence of philosophy, combined with the superiority which is attributed to the judge who "forces himself," ever defended by the ruling power, could not but exacerbate his Maliki colleagues. They finally succeeded in exiling Averroës to Lucena in 1195.[44] This exile underscored the end of the serendipitous balance, fruit of pragmatic wisdom as well as the spiritual finesse of those whom Averroës praised as able to call both elite and people to assume their place in a community of "true Muslims" (Qur'an 2:22).

Conclusion

Returning to the principles which structure the dual role of the philosophico-religious debate we have been following, let us consider three points. First, the way the evidence which faith gives to both Ghazali and Averroës in the existence of a Creator criss-crosses with their diverse experience of reason. What results from this criss-crossing are two ways of affirming the perfection of the created universe. And this manifest difference can help us distinguish these two thinkers by their respective visions of a well-ordered society, designed to preserve the essentials of Qur'anic revelation. Ghazali could have found a place, albeit subordinate, in the heterogeneous society which Averroës proposed; whereas he himself would have had no place in the homogeneous society of believers to which Ghazali aspired. Finally, we must note a conviction shared by both protagonists, though for different reasons: that religious debate ought not be aired in public. This very vision will help us appreciate ways in which their times resemble our own.

Both Ghazali and Averroës averred a chasm separating God from creatures in their totality which constitutes the world, yet at the same time a strict connection obtains at the very heart of being between the Agent and His works. And both identify the task proper to human beings as one of recognizing this relation of dependence without attenuating divine transcendence. Finally, both find human reason to be limited, and locate our recognition of the transcendent existence of God and so the ultimate perfection of human beings in our awareness of these limits. So the key question then becomes one of the limits of this limitation. How far can one accentuate the limits of reason and of the world without affecting the excellence of reasoning its ability to recognize the transcendence of God, on the one hand, and the excellence of the world as it testifies to the omnipotence of its Author on the other? Averroës and Ghazali part company on this point.

Averroës is convinced that the causal relation is at once essential and sufficiently ample to indicate both the unique connection between Creator and creatures, and the excellence of the work of art which is the world. The philosopher exploits the image of the Artisan, proposing to preserve His unicity by the roles which matter will play with respect to specific existents that He alone is able to fashion. In this way, the philosopher-believer hopes to preserve both the fact of knowledge as well as its proper limit: composition of created things. For no knowledge of God is possible without appreciating how our ability to know is limited to specific existents. The fullness of existence is only revealed to us in a way that is affected and limited by the essences of what we can properly know. For it is precisely as composed and perfectly ordered that reality points to the Totally Other whose intention divides, composes and orders form and matter as well as the entirety of natural substances.

Ghazali aligns himself against this solution which he finds diminishes the Author in the name of preserving the intelligibility of the work itself. He locates the role of reason in recognizing what is possible, but in the immense ocean so unveiled, reason can only get lost. For reality cannot establish itself nor can reason found it; the unique founder is God, the Agent whose absolutely free will is the only true cause. Nevertheless, without pretending to be privy to the divine "measuring out," which traces the connection of real things with the possibility which grounds them, Ghazali insists that human beings can know that God does not choose randomly. While infinitely free, God chooses in line with His perfection, following to the ninety-nine names of God as the pinnacle of moral perfection to which we aspire. Our world is distinguished from any other "possible world" by the fullness of perfection which it displays as well as the progress which we can make in imitating the ultimate Perfection which is His. So the more we progress on this route, the better we will appreciate the choice which is His. So we can see how both protagonists affirm the supreme excellence of what is, whether by the path of God's free choice or by the creative intention of the Artisan.

It is Averroës' intimate conviction that nothing can disturb the perfect order of the world or the utter coherence of the precious Book. Yet he fears the bad effect which certain people can have on those who, while not being "people of demonstration," are no longer simple believers confirmed in their faith. Such people will pose questions, and inadequate responses may well tarnish their outlook on the world, disturb their certitude in the perspicuous Word, and so lead them astray in their actions. The fact that human beings can deceive themselves, and so bring disarray to others without any evil intent on their part, only exacerbates the problem.

Averroës feels that this is the case with Ghazali, an extremely gifted spiritual master who is allowed to propose a theory of interpretation of revelation, as well as delineate the precise sense of articles of faith, yet without being a philosopher. At the same time, how precious might have been the teaching of a more responsible spiritual guide, better aware of his own limits! By restricting his interventions to believers who are "people of rhetoric," such a spiritual guide could take the opportunity of verses regarding the "ascent" of God onto the throne to deepen the reverential awe before the One on whom all that is depends, and who addresses Himself to human beings by using images fitted to them.

Let me emphasize that Averroës, as believing philosopher, proposed the image of Artisan in this very spirit. Addressing himself to "people of demonstration," he hoped simply to enhance the perception that everything which exists depends on God, the unique Creator, whose essence is to exist. Moreover, he is convinced that particular images are suited to each constituency, adapted to their degree of knowledge, yet Ghazali revolted against this very presumption. For him, espousing religiously relevant categorical differences among human beings, according to their degrees of knowing, simply displays the hypocrisy of philosophers, full of themselves, jugglers of concepts, convinced they are privy to God's own "measuring out." For Ghazali, when philosophers are so convinced of their own superiority as interpreters of revelation as to concede a subalternate place to spiritual masters, they only display their unbelief.

For what could be meant by the Law if not equality of believers, all equally distant from the perfection of the Creator? How can one utilize knowledge of Aristotle with his distinctions, to turn one's nose up at traits shared by all human beings? Indeed, as we have seen, the very heart of Ghazali's teaching involved clarifying these shared features. The ephemeral, infinitely evasive thirst for power, which tyrannizes all of us, is at the center of his *Revivication of Religious Learning*. Fear and hope for the final ends trace the uniquely worthwhile path, shared by servants of God aware of their unworthiness. The respective visions available to a society of believers allow us to measure the sharp disagreement setting Averroës against Ghazali. Yet this very disagreement will help us appreciate the solution which both proffered to neutralize the dangers which public discussion of matters of faith portends.

Neither Ghazali nor Averroës would countenance broaching the questions we have considered here in the public domain. Once in the public arena, such discussions could only create misunderstanding and stir up discord, so helping to obscure what is essential. Averroës would have reminded us of the duty of silence which he believes philosophical skills impose. Given the radical differences separating non-philosophers from philosophers, he would regard those lacking philosophical skill as prone to work mischief on all sides, unable as they are to comprehend the issues at stake. Yet Ghazali spoke of what is essential to faith, emphasizing the religious dimension of our subject. So how have we contributed to the one thing necessary, fear and hope before the Eternal, in proposing this counterpoint between philosophy and common sense?

Yet this spirited exchange, which we have followed to the very point of convergence between the two protagonists regarding the noxious effects of public discussion of philosophical-religious subjects, could effectively remind us of things we tend to forget. From our vantage point in the twenty-first century, divisions can no longer be accentuated in the name of universal human equality; while dialogue is encouraged among the three great monotheisms in the name of Revelation, yet we might forget that human beings have not changed that much. Indeed, we might be instructed by the polemical exchange initiated by the conference of Pope Benedict XVI, formerly (as Cardinal Ratzinger) prefect of the Congregation for the Doctrine of the Faith, to see how well-founded is the position of Ghazali and Averroës proscribing public discussion of these matters. Delivered on September 12, 2007 at the University of Regensburg, both defenders and detractors of the sovereign pontiff seemed quite comfortable associating cardinal-professor with the Pope (www.vatican.va/ [accessed 31 March 200]). Yet detractors objected to the Pope employing a maladroit and divisive example to make his point, while defenders remarked on the finesse of his presentation. Detractors followed Ghazali to insist that, as Pope, Benedict XVI ought only speak of essentials shared by all human beings before the Eternal. Defenders, like Averroës, deplored the wrong done by subtle intellectual distinctions meant for an elite who could understand them, once these distinctions were broadcast to the uninstructed as well.

Ought one simply keep silence about matters like these which can unsettle people, renounce dialogue altogether and squelch the desire to understand? Given the subtleties involved in knowing what to say in a fashion as clear as it is humble, one should acknowledge that Benedict XVI spoke in service of his vision of human flourishing, while our ability to listen to divergent opinions, without needing to take offense or put the other down, names the heart of our present situation. But that goes well beyond the limits of this counterpoint, by which I hope to have succeeded in clarifying the non-monolithic character of the religion of the Book par excellence.

Notes

1 Journeys of Ghazali and Averroës to their diverse conceptions of the role of reason

1 Cf. M. Hogga, "Orthodoxie, subversion et réforme en Islam," *Etudes musulmanes* 34 (1933) 214–20; Abbas Muhajirani, "Twelve Shi'ite Imams," in *History of Islamic Philosophy*, eds. Sayyed Hossein Nasr and Oliver Leaman (London: Routledge, 1996) 119–43.

2 This subject has been amply treated by D. Gutas, *Greek Thought Arabic Culture, The Graeco-Arabic Translation Movement in Baghdad and early Abbasid Society* (London: Routledge, 1998).

3 *Encyclopedia of Islam.* 2: 1038–41; M. Campanini, "Al-Ghazali" in *Introduction to Islamic Philosophy*, tr. Caroline Higgitt (Edinburgh: Edinburgh University Press, 2008). 258–76; Farid Jabre, *Al-Munqid min Adâlal* [Erreur et délivrance] trad. française avec traduction et notes, 2ème éd. (Beirut, 1969) 15–52; ET: W.M. Watt, *The Faith and Practice of Al-Ghazali* (London: G. Allen and Unwin, 1967) at 11.

4 F. Jabre, *La vie et l'œuvre de Ghazali reconsidérées à la lumière des Tabaqât de Subki* (Cairo: Institut dominicain d'études orientales [IDEO], 1954) I, 76–82; M. L. Siauve, *L'amour de Dieu chez Ghazali* (Paris: Vrin, 1986) 4–5, 59–66.

5 F. Jabre, *Al-Munqidh*, op. cit, Introduction, 18–19.

6 D. Burrell, "Avicenna," in *Companion to Philosophy in the Middle Ages*, ed. by J. J. E. Gracia and T. B. Loone (Oxford: Blackwell, 2003) 196–208, at 198.

7 H. Dabashi, "Ayn al-Qudât Hamadanni and The Intellectual Climate at His Times," in *History of Islamic Philosophy*, ed. by S. H. Nasr and O. Leaman (London: Routledge, 1996) 374–433.

8 *Encyclopedia of Islam*, vol. 2, 1039–41; R. J. McCarthy, *Freedom and Fulfillment* (Boston: Twayne Publishers, 1980) xxix–xlii; Farhad Dartary, *The Isma'ilis: Their History and Doctrine* (Cambridge: Cambridge University Press, 1990) 324 ff.

9 According to M. Hogga,

> lorsque l'environnement de Ghazali devint la négation de sa fonction politico-pédagogique, il activa l'émergence d'une rupture jusque-là sous-jacente entre l'idéal éthique islamique et la pratique du pouvoir

chez le théologien (. . .). Les facteurs structurels de cette crise résident dans la contradiction entre une socialisation soufie (lors de l'enfance) et une formation intellectuelle dans la *Nizamiyya* . . ." ("Orthodoxie . . ., (op. cit, 156–7).

10 Averroes, *The book of the Decisive Treatise Determining the Connection Between the Law and Wisdom with Epistle Dedicatory* tr. Charles Butterworth (Provo, YT: Brigham Young University Press, 2001) at 1.

11 Averroes, *Decisive Treatise*, tr. Butterworth (Provo: Brigham Young University Press, 2001) 32–3. I find the praise of the Almohades which ends the *Decisive Treatise* to be both sincere and amply justified, as I have explained in Chapter 6. For a developed argument that this praise "seems to contain more than a suspicion of sarcasm," see Sarah Stroumza, "Philosophes almohades? Averroès, Maïmonide et l'idéologie almohade," in *Los Almohades: Problemas y perspectivas*, vol. II, Patrice Cressier Maribel Fierro y Louis Molina (eds.), Estudios arabes e islamicos, monografias, 2005) 1137–62, cité 1149, § 1.

12 M. Cruz Hernández, "La crítica de Averroes al despotismo oligárquico andaluz," in *Al Encuentro de Averroes*, ed. A. M. Lorca, Madrid, Editorial Trotta, 1993. Cf. M. Geoffroy, "L'almohadisme théologique d'Averroès," in *Archives d'histoire doctrinale et littéraire du Moyen Age* 66 (1999) 9–47.

13 *Decisive Treatise*, par. 72, note 11.

14 D. Urvoy, *Ibn Rushd*, tr. O. Stewart (London: Routledge, 1991) 10, 16.

15 D. Urvoy, *Le monde des oulémas andalous du V/XIème au VII/XIIIème siècles* (Genève, 1978) 129–31.

16 Roger Arnaldez, *A Rationalist in Islam*, tr. D. Streight (Notre Dame, IN: University of Notre Dame Press, 2000) 7.

17 Arnaldez, 8.

18 Chapter 4.

19 Averroes, *On the Harmony of Religion and Philosophy* tr. George Hourani (London: Luzac & Co. Ltd., 1960) at 9.

20 D. Urvoy, "La pensée d'Ibn Tûmart," in *Bulletin d'études orientales*, XXVII (Damas, 1974) 19–24; M. Geoffroy, "L'almohadisme théologique d'Averroès," op. cit., 13–17.

21 J. Puig, "Materials on Averroes's circle," *Journal of Near Eastern Studies* 51 (1992) 241–60.

22 Translation by Lenn Goodman (Los Angeles: Gee Tee Bee, 1976).

23 Averroës, *On the Harmony of Religion and Philosophy* tr. George Hourani (London: Luzac & Co. Ltd., 1960) 12–13. *Bidaya al-Mujtahid Commencement pour qui s'efforce . . . courts commentaires sur l'Organon d'Aristote: la Physique et la Métaphysique, Les parties des animaux, De la génération et de la corruption.*

24 M. Geoffroy, "L'almohadisme théologique," op. cit., 11–12, 11, note 6.

25 I. Goldziher, Introduction à D. Luciani (éd.), *Le livre de Mohammed ibn Tûmart, Mahdi des Almohades* (Alger, 1903) 1.

26 S. Pinès, "Philosophy," *The Cambridge History of Islam*, P. M. Holt *et al.* eds (Cambridge: Cambridge University Press:, 1970) vol. 2, 814–15; M. Geoffroy, "L'almohadisme théologique . . .," op. cit., p. 47.

27 S. Stroumsa, "Philosophes almohades? Averroès . . .," op. cit., 6–7, 10. The

author maintains that "the metaphysical preoccupations typical of philosophers seems far from the intellectual agenda of the Almohades" (1143). She explains the contrary testimony from the conversation between Averroës and Abu Yacub as follows:

> Even were one to accept this account as veridical, there is no reason to suppose that the caliph would raise the issue in philosophical terms in the absence of Averroës (1144). Yet the issue may be moot, given the specialized interest which this author finds the caliph to have had in Averroës: "the caliph was only interested in examining a candidate recommended for his service. . . . Averroës had been recruited for high administrative posts in the state" (1141–2).

28 M. Fakhry, *Averroes, His life . . .*, op. cit, (Oxford: One World, 2001) 2.

29 Ibid.

30 My basic disagreement with Marc Geoffroy's contention that Averroës had succeeded in restoring Ibn Tûmart's conception of divine transcendence to assist his own "project of secularizing philosophical discourse" (M. Geoffroy, "L'almohadisme théologique . . .," op. cit 10, 47) will emerge in Chapter 5 of this book.

31 M. Geoffroy, "L'almohadisme . . .," ibid., 12; D. Urvoy, op.cit., 34–6; M. Fakhry, *Averroès . . .*, op. cit., 2–3.

32 G. F. Hourani, Averroes, *On the Harmony of Religion and Philosophy* (London: Luzac,1976) 1.

33 Ibid., 19.

34 Ibid., 11, 13.

35 Ibid., 18, note 6; A. de Libera, *Le Livre du discours décisif* (Paris: Flammarion, 1996) 11, notes 13, 14.

36 De Libera, ibid., 6.

37 Hourani, *Averroes, op. cit.*, 25–26; 38, note 3.

38 Libera, *Discours décisif*, op. cit., Introduction, 56–69.

39 Hourani, op. cit., 39.

40 Hourani, ibid., 38.

41 Hourani, ibid., 38.

42 Hourani, Ibid., 39.

43 B. S. Kogan, *Averroes and the Metaphysics of Causation* (Albany, NY: State University of New-York Press, 1985) Chapter 2.

44 M. Allard, "Le rationalisme d'Averroès d'après une étude sur la Création," *Bulletin d'études orientales*, no. 14, 1952–4, 7–59, (Damas Institut français: de Damas, 1954), 20–7; cf. also Hourani, op. cit., 39, notes 2 and 3.

45 M. Geoffroy, "L'almohadisme . . .," op. cit., 10, 47.

46 R. Arnaldez, *A Rationalist in Islam*, op. cit., 2.

47 M. Fakhri, *Averroes, His life . . .*, op. cit., Introduction, vxi.

48 I. A. Bello, *The Medieval Islamic Controversy between Philosophy and Orthodoxy* (Leiden: E. J. Brill, 1989). 12, 142, 143, 144, 146 and151.

49 *Zandaqa*, a translation adopted at the suggestion of Sherman A. Jackson in his Introduction to his translation: *On the Boundaries of Theological tolerance in Islam*, Studies in Islamic Philosophy, ed. S. Nomanul Haq (Karachi: Oxford University Press, 2002). 55–9.

50 W. M. Watt, "Al-Ghazali," *Encyclopedia of Islam*, vol. 2, p. 1040.

51 R. Frank, *Al-Ghazali and the Asharite School* (Durham, NC: Duke University Press, 1994) 78.
52 M. Hogga, "Orthodoxie, subversion et réforme en Islam," op. cit. 25.
53 Ibid., 176–7.
54 I. Goldziher, *Vorlesung über den Islam* (Heidelberg, 1910) cited by Jackson, *On the Boundaries . . .*, op. cit, 40, following the translation of M. Swartz in G. Makdisi, *Hanabalite Islam, Studies on Islam*, tr. and ed. by M. Swarz (Oxford, Oxford University Press, 1981) 80, note 97.
55 I. A. Bello, op. cit. 146.
56 Jackson, op. cit 74.
57 Ibid., 40.
58 Ibid., 51–2.
59 H. Lazarus-Yafeh, *Studies in al-Ghazali* (Jerusalem: The Magnes Press of Hebrew University, 1973) 437–57; M. Whittingham, "Al-Ghazali on Jews and Christians," in B. Roggema, M. Poorthuis and P. Valkenberg, *The Three Rings*, (Leuven: Peeters, 2005) [Publications of the Thomas Institute, Utrecht, New Series, vol. XI] 204–16, esp. 207, 215 and 216.

2 From the chimera of philosophy to the evidence of "The Just Balance"

1 Hava Lazarus-Yafeh, *Studies in al-Ghazali*, (Hebrew University of Jerusalem: The Magnes Press, 1975).
2 H. Lazarus-Yafeh, ibid., 3; Chapters 1, 18; Chapter 2, 50.
3 Ibid., Chapter 2, note 11, 213.
4 W. M. Watt, *Al-Ghazali, Encyclopedia of Islam Vol. II.*, 1040; M.-L. Siauve, *L'amour de Dieu chez Ghazali*, (Paris: Vrin, 1986) 64; M. Hogga, "Orthodoxie, subversion et réforme en Islam," *Études musulmanes* 34 (1933) 17.
5 Lazarus-Yafeh, op. cit., Chapter VII; cf. aussi Mohamed Arkoun, "Révélation, vérité et histoire d'après l'œuvre de Ghazali," in *Essais sur la pensée islamique*, (Paris: Maisonneuve & Larose, 1973) 239.
6 Lazarus-Yafeh, ibid., Chapter 2, 87.
7 Ibid., Chapter 2, 84–113; 130–50.
8 Ibid., Chapter 2, 87.
9 Ibid., Chapter 2, 85 and note 64, 223.
10 Sayyed Mohammed Khatami, *La religion et la pensée prises au piège de l'autocratie*, (Louvain-Paris: Peeters, 2005) 110–11.
11 Lazarus-Yafeh, op. cit., Chapter 2, 178–80.
12 Lazarus-Yafeh, ibid., Chapter 5, 349 and 351; cf. also Chapters 4, 266.
13 F. Jabre, *La notion de la Maarifa chez Ghazali*, (Beirut: Dar El Machreq, 2ème éd.,1986).
14 Ghazali, *The Incoherence of the Philosophers*, a parallel English-Arabic text translated, introduced and annotated by Michael E. Marmura, (Provo, UT: Brigham Young University Press, 2000) Introduction, 16.
15 M.-L. Siauve, *L'amour de Dieu . . .*, op. cit., 14.
16 Shams Inati, "Logic," in *History of Islamic Philosophy*, edited by Sayyed Hossein Nasr and Oliver Leaman, Routledge, 1996, Chapters 48, 802–23.
17 Ibid., 805–6, notes 19–22.

18 Ibid., 806, notes 24 et 25.
19 Ibid.,822, note 74.
20 Ibid., p. 822, notes 82, 86 et 87.
21 M. Marmura, op. cit., p. 1.
22 Ibid., 2.
23 Ibid., 3.
24 Ibid., 4.
25 Ibid., 5.
26 Cf. M. Allard, *Le problème des attributs divins dans la doctrine d'Achari*, (Beirut: Imprimerie catholique, 1965).
27 Ibid., 5.
28 Ibid.
29 Ibid., 7.
30 Ibid.
31 Ibid., 8–10.
32 Ibid., 59.
33 Cf. Marmura, op. cit., note 1, 244.
34 Ibid., 227; note 1., 244.
35 Ibid., 226
36 "La Revivification des sciences de la religion," (Beirut, 1420/1982), cited by Sayyed Mohammed Khatami in *La religion et la pensée prises au piège de l'autocratie*, op. cit., 115–16.
37 R. J. McCarthy, *Freedom and Fulfillment* (Boston: Twayne Publishers, 1980), 91; *Al-Ghazali's Deliverance from Error* (Louisville, KY: Fons Vitae, 2005) 79.
38 "La Revivification . . .," cited by Khatami, op. cit., 116.
39 "La Revivification . . .," 4ème Livre, traité 38, in G. H. Bousquet, "Du contrôle spirituel et de l'examen de conscience," tome 6, 2750, cited by M. Hogga, "Orthodoxie . . .," op. cit., 185.
40 "La Revivification . . .," fasc. "Kitab Asrar al Zakat" (Le mystère de l'impôt religieux). Tome 1, 389, cited by M. Hogga, ibid., 183.
41 M.-L. Siauve, *L'amour de Dieu . . .*, op. cit., 75.
42 F. Jabre, *La notion de la Maarifa chez Ghazali*, op. cit., 39–62.
43 "La Revivification . . .,"op. cit., p. 243 ss., cf. F. Jabre, ibid., pp. 56–7, see Appendix 8, pp. 189sq for Arabic text.
44 M.-L. Siauve, *L'amour de Dieu . . .*, op. cit., 34; M. Hogga, "Orthodoxie . . .," op. cit., 25.
45 W. M. Watt, *The Faith and Practice of Al-Ghazali* (London: G. Allen and Unwin, 1967) at 52.
46 Ibid.
47 M. Hogga, op. cit.,174.
48 M.-L. Siauve, op. cit.,47.
49 (*Qistas Al Mustaqim* ("La Balance Juste"), éd. Taraqqi, (Cairo, 1318/1900); éd. Victor-Chelhot, (Beirut, 1959); trad. française de Victor Chelhot, in *Bulletin d'Études orientales*, XV, 7–98.
50 Ibid., 44.
51 Ibid., 45–6.
52 Cf. Qur'an 6:83: "this is the decisive argument we have given to Abraham against his people." See *Qistas . . .*, op. cit., pp. 52–4.

53 *Qistas . . .*, ibid., Chapter II, 52–4.
54 *Qistas . . .*, ibid., Chapter III, 55.
55 *Qistas . . .*, ibid., Chapter IV, 59.

3 The decisive criterion of the distinction between Islam and hypocrisy (zandaqa)

1 *Al-Ghazali's Deliverance from Error* (Louisville, KY: Fons Vitae, 2005) 91.
2 Ibid.
3 Sherman A. Jackson, *On the Boundaries of Theological Tolerance in Islam*, Studies in Islamic Philosophy, Nomanul Haq (Karachi: Oxford University Press, 2002) p. 56: "Al-Ghazali's concern was rather with unbelief that attempted to pass itself off as falling within the boundaries of Islam."
4 Ibid., p. 57 and notes 121, 122.
5 *Livre de la crainte et de l'espérance*, éd. Halabi, Livre 33, tome IV, p. 137, ET: *Ghazal's Book of Fear and Hope*, tr. William McKane (Leiden: Brill, 1962).
6 Ibid., p. 156.
7 Cf. M.-L. Siauve, *L'amour de Dieu chez Ghazali*, op. cit., pp. 211–26.
8 S. A. Jackson, op. cit., p. 40
9 Ibid., p. 66.
10 Cf. M.-L. Siauve, op. cit., pp. 211–15.
11 Translator's note: since the author worked with M. Hogga, *Le critère décisif de distinction entre l'islam et le manichéisme* (Bordeaux: Bibliothèque universitaire, 1983), which sometimes differs from the English translation of Sherman A. Jackson, *On the Boundaries of Theological Tolerance in Islam*, Studies in Islamic Philosophy, Nomanul Haq (Karachi: Oxford University Press, 2002), for consistency with the original, I utilize sometimes one translation and sometimes another, noting the pagination for each in parentheses in the text: B = *Boundaries*; C = *Critère*; so here (B92, C19).

4 Averroës, philosopher-reader of the precious Book

1 Composed in 1179, trans. G.-F. Hourani, *Averroës, On the Harmony . . .*, op. cit., 76–8.
2 *The incoherence of the incoherence*, translation with introduction and notes by Simon Van den Bergh, 2 vols., (London: Luzac & Co., 1954).
3 G.-F. Hourani, *On the Harmony of Religion and Philosophy*, E. J. W. Gibb Memorial Series, New Series, XXI, 1976, 72–81.
4 Averroës, *The Book of the Decisive Treatise Determining the Connection Between the Law and Wisdom and Epistle Dedicatory*, tr. Butterworth (Provo, UT: Brigham Young University Press, 2001) at 1.
5 Averroës, *Decisive Treatise*, tr. Butterworth, 1–2.
6 Aristotle, *Métaphysics*, Bk. Delta, Chapter 4 (1015 a 15).
7 *Al-Kashf an Marahiij al-Adilla* (*Le livre de l'exposition des méthodes de la preuve*), (Beirut: Dar el-Afaq ad-Jahida, 1402 h/1982) 63–4, cited in *Discours décisif*, 176, note 3.
8 Ibid., 70. Cf. *Discours décisif*, op. cit., 176, note 3.
9 Averroës, *Decisive Treatise*, tr. Butterworth, 2.

10 Averroës, *Decisive Treatise*, tr. Butterworth, 2–3.

11 Averroës, *Decisive Treatise* tr. Butterworth, 2–3.

12 "We must note that what particularly recommends using the rhetorical syllogism is its capacity to convince without even suggesting contrary possibilities, though these may be just as probable as the conclusion the orator seeks to impose." Averroës, *Decisive Treatise* tr. Butterworth, 24–5.

13 "Averroës gives special attention to juridical syllogisms which conclude to laws, whose precise recommendations are similar to the rational syllogisms of philosophers."
Averroës, *Decisive Treatise* tr. Butterworth, 3–4.

14 "Restricted to the practical order, they vary with circumstances of time and place."
Averroës, *Decisive Treatise* tr. Butterworth, 11.

15 Ibid., § 20, note 51, 190–1.

16 Ibid., § 7, note 20, 182.

17 Averroës, *Decisive Treatise* tr. Butterworth, 8.

18 Averroës, *Decisive Treatise* tr. Butterworth, 8.

19 Averroës, *Decisive Treatise* tr. Butterworth, 22.

20 This community involves those for whom philosophical inquiry is a vital necessity: "to deny the study of philosophical works to those so endowed . . . is no less than denying a thirsty person a drink of fresh cold water, lest he die of thirst. . . ." Averroës, *Decisive Treatise* tr. Butterworth, 7.

21

> Now since this Revelation is the truth, and it invites us to practice rational examination which can assure knowledge of the truth, it follows that we Muslims know with a certain knowledge that the examination [of beings] by demonstration can in no way contradict the teachings of the revealed text, because truth cannot contradict truth, but accords with it and gives witness on its behalf.
>
> (Averroës, *Decisive Treatise*, 8–9)

22 For

> what we do in interpreting is to move the meaning of a word from its proper sense to a figurative one, without distorting the way the Arabic language uses figurative language: anything can de designated by its analogue, its cause, its effect, its complement, or other recognized tropes.
>
> (Averroës, *Decisive Treatise* tr. Butterworth, 9)

23 Dominique Urvoy, *Averroès, les ambitions d'un intellectuel musulman*, coll. Grandes biographies, (Paris: Flammarion, 1998),161.

24 "If they agree, nothing more need be said; if they contradict each other, we can always interpret the plain sense." Averroës, *Decisive Treatise* tr. Butterworth, 9, 25.

25

> We can categorically insist that wherever a contradiction may arise between the results of demonstration and the plain sense of a revelational statement, that statement can be interpreted according to the rules of interpretation [in conformity with the usage] of the Arabic language.
>
> (Averroës, *Decisive Treatise* tr. Butterworth, 9)

26 Ibid.
27 Ibid., § 22.
28 Ibid., § 23.
29 Cited by Averroës, ibid.
30 Ibid., § 28.
31 Ibid.
32 *The Incoherence of the Philosophers.* A parallel English-Arabic text translation, introduced and annotated by M.-E. Marmura, (Provo, UT: Brigham Young University Press: Provo, 2000) conclusion, note 1, 244.
33 Cf. *Discours Décisif*, notes 59, 67 and 68.
34 Ibid., § 27.
35 Barry S. Kogan, *Averroës and the Metaphysics of Causation*, (Albany: State University of New York Press, 1985).
36 Ibid., 7.
37 *Tahafut al-Falasifa*, p. 520, *Tahafut al-Tahafut*, p. 406. Cf. B. S. Kogan, op. cit., Chapter 3, 98, n 36. Ghazali, *Tahafut al-Falasifa* (*L'incohérence des philosophes*), Arabic text accompanied by a Latin synopsis and index by Maurice Bouyges, (Bibliotheca Arabica Scholasticorum, Série arabe, t. II, Beirut: Imprimerie catholique, 1927). Averroës, *Tahafut al-Tahafut* (*The Incoherence of the Incoherence*), translated with introduction and notes by Simon Van den Bergh (London: Luzac & Co., 1934).
38 *Discours décisif*, § 27.
39 Ibid., § 29, note 71. We shall consider this subject in the fifth chapter: *the Producer* (*al-Bari*), *the Hidden* (*al-Batin*).
40 Aristotle, *Métaphysics*, Bk. Delta 4 (1015 a 14–15).
41 *Discours décisif*, § 29.
42 Ibid., § 27.
43 Ibid., § 29.
44 Ibid., § 30.
45 G.-F. Hourani, Averroës, *On the Harmony*, op. cit., 72–5. Cf. *Discours décisif*, note 74, 199.
46 *Discours décisif*, § 31.
47 Ibid.
48 Ibid., note 76, 199.
49 Ibid., § 32, *Discours décisif*, note 80, 200.
50 Ibid., § 32, *Discours décisif*, note 80, 200.
51 Ibid.
52 Ibid., § 33.
53 Aristotle, *Physics*, IV, 11, (220 a 24–6).
54 *Discours décisif*, § 34.
55 Ibid., § 39.
56 Ibid., § 43.
57 Ibid., § 45. Cf. *Discours décisif*, note 110, 207.
58 *Kitab al-Kashf* (*Le livre de l'exposition*), 122–7. G.-F. Hourani, Averroës. *On the harmony*, op. cit., 76–8.
59 Hourani, ibid., p. 76; *Kitab al-Kashf*, ibid., p. 122.
60 *Kitab al-Kashf*, ibid., 123; Hourani, ibid., 77.
61 *Kitab al-Kashf*, ibid., p. 122; Hourani, ibid., 76.
62 *Kitab al-Kashf*, ibid., 123–5; Hourani, ibid., note 217, p. 119.

63 *Averroës, L'intelligence et la pensée, sur le De anima*, presentation and translation by Alain de Libera (Paris: Garnier-Flammarion, 1998), where Averroës
poses a precise question regarding the proper subject of thought, as psychic or
immaterial, 39.

5 Reorganization of the world according to Aristotle in the light of Qur'anic revelation by Averroës

1 J. Jolivet, "Divergences entre les métaphysiques d'Ibn Rushd et d'Aristote,"
Arabica, no. 29, 1982, 225–45; Ch. Touati, *Multiple Averroès* (Paris, 1978),
161; D. Urvoy, *Ibn Rushd (Averroès)*, trans. O. Stewart, op. cit., pp. 38, 104,
106.
2 D.-W. Graham, *Aristotle's Two Systems*, (Oxford: Clarendon Press, 1987);
M.-L. Gill, *Aristotle on Substance, The Paradox of Unity* (Princeton:
Princeton University Press, 1989).
3 Graham, op. cit., 287.
4 Gill, op. cit., 242.
5 Graham, op. cit., Chapter 8; Gill, ibid., Chapter 1.
6 Gill, ibid., 240–2.
7 Graham, ibid., Chapter 9.
8 Gill., ibid., 203, 209–10, 225.
9 Graham, ibid., Chapters 2, 4 and 8.
10 Ibid., 264–78, cf. 276, note 32.
11 Gill, ibid., Chapters 1, 38–40; Chapters 2, 7 and Appendix.
12 Aristotle, *Metaphysics* (A. 1) 980 a 1.
13 *Nichomachean Ethics* (10. 8) 1178 b 22.
14 Graham, op. cit., 287.
15 Ibn Rushd's *Metaphysics*. A translation with introduction of Ibn Rushd's
Commentary on Aristotle's Metaphysics, Book Lam, by Ch. Genequand, (J.
Brill: Leiden, 1984). § 1736 line 6, p. 210.
16 The tension at the heart of Aristotle's system between natural generation
according to eternally subsistent species, and "spontaneous generation" is var-
iously interpreted today. Cf. A. Gotthalf, "Aristotle's conception of final
causality," in A. Gotthalf and J.-G. Lennox, editors, *Philosophical Issues in
Aristotle's Biology*, (Cambridge: Cambridge University Press, 1987)
199–223; J.-M. Cooper, "Hypothetical Necessity and Natural Teleology," in
A. Gotthalf andJ.-G. Lennox, editors, ibid., 243–74; J.-G. Lennox,
"Teleology, Chance and Aristotle's Theory of Spontaneous Generation," in
Journal of the History of Philosophy, no. 20, 219–38.
17 Averroës, *De Substantia Orbis*, critical edition of the Hebrew text with
English translation and commentary, by Arthur Hyman (Cambridge:
Cambridge University Press, 1986).
18 *De Substantia Orbis*, ibid., Chapters 1, 24 (page references refer to the texts
redacted in Hebrew, included within the work itself).
19 Ibid., Chapters 1, 13
20 Ibid., Chapters 1, 14.
21 Ibid., Chapter 1, p. 20; Chapter 2, p. 31.
22 Ibid., column 1474, § 1–5. *Commentary on Aristotle's Metaphysics*, book
lamda, col. 1474.

23 *Commentary on Aristotle's Metaphysics*, book lamda, col. 1444–6.
24 *Commentary on Aristotle's Metaphysics*, book lamda col. 1449. Book delta, 1069 b 26.
25 *Commentary on Aristotle's Metaphysics*, book lamda, col. 1449, § 4–7.
26 *L'intention première: àla-l'-qasd al-awwal. Commentary on Aristotle's Metaphysics* book lamda, col. 1460, lines 8–9. See Genequand, op. cit., Introduction, Chapter 3, p. 25, note 2. The primary intention moves the existing whole as both form and finality. Ibid., col. 1425 and 1434. Its activity and its products form a unity. Ibid., col. 1529.
27 *Commentary on Aristotle's Metaphysics*, book lamda, col. 1472–5.
28 *De Substantia Orbis*, op. cit., Chapter 3, 46–7; Chapters 6, 53.
29 Ibid., Chapters 2, 34; Chapter 3, p. 42 and 47.
30 Ibid., Chapter 1, p. 22; Chapter 5, p. 50.
31 Ibid., Chapters 1, 23; Chapters 6, 53.
32 Ibid., Chapters 1, 24.
33 Ibid.
34 Ibid., Chapters 2, 29.
35 Ibid.
36 *Métaphysics*, book lamda 3 (1070 a 5); Averroës, Comm., col. 1456–95.
37 Aristotle, *Prior Analytics*, 24 b 22.
38 Aristotle, *History of Animals*, 588 b 455.
39 Aristotle, *Parts of Animals*, 681 a 955.
40 *History of Animals*, Chapter 15, 569 a 10–569 b 10; *Generation of Animals*, 762 b 28.
41 *Commentary on Aristotle's Metaphysics*, book lamda., col. 1456–95.
42 *Commentary on Aristotle's Metaphysics*, book lamda, col. 1425.
43 Ibid., col. 1429–36.
44 Ibid., col. 1425, 1434, 1460.
45 Ibid., col. 1529.
46 Ibid., comm. col. 1461.
47 Ibid., comm. col. 1458, 1460.
48 Ibid., col. 1457.
49 Ibid., col. 1464.
50 Ibid., col. 1494–5; 1498–9.
51 Ibid., col. 1495.
52 Ibid., col. 1530.
53 *Al-umur al-sinaiyya* (*Les produits artisanaux*), comm. col. 1495, § 9.
54 *Commentary on Aristotle's Metaphysics*, book lamda. col. 1463–4.
55 Ibid., col. 1632.
56 For a contrary opinion, see L. Bauloye (Lüttich), "Note sur la doctrine rusch-dienne de la substance, d'après le Grand Commentaire de la Métaphysique," in *Averroes (1126–1198) oder der Triumph der rationalismus*, Internationales Symposium, Heidelberg, October 1998; ed. Raif Georges Khoury (Heidelberg, 2002) 233–42.
57 *Commentary on Aristotle's Metaphysics*, book lamda, 1620–1.
58 Ibid., col. 1622.
59 Ibid., col. 1505.
60 Ibid., col. 1707–8.
61 Ibid., col. 1708–9; cf. ibid., col. 1698, 1703 and 1704.

62 *De Substantia Orbis*, op. cit., Chapters 2, 32.
63 *Commentary on Aristotle's Metaphysics*, book lamda, 1505. In his commentary on *De Coelo* I, c. 90, Averroës clarifies that failure to realize the impossible can hardly diminish the excellence of the First., cf. A. de Libera, *Averroès, L'intelligence et la pensée*, notes 185, 215.
64 *Commentary on Aristotle's Metaphysics*, book lamda, col. 1727, § 6; cf. ibid., col. 1734.
65 Qur'an, 15, 26–43.
66 *Commentary on Aristotle's Metaphysics*, book lamda, col. 1617, § 4–8.
67 Ibid., col. 1611.9–1613.
68 Ibid., col. 1593.
69 Plato, *Laws* 645 a.
70 Ibid.
71 Plato, *Republic* (book 10), 619.
72 Plotinus, *Enneads*, I. 6, 9, 13.
73 Ibid., VI, 4, 14, 16.
74 Aristotle, *Metaphysics*, book lamda 10, 1075 a 11–15.
75 *Commentary on Aristotle's Metaphysics*, book lamda, col. 1711.
76 *Commentary on Aristotle's Metaphysics*, book lamda, col. 1713.
77 Ibid., col. 1715. Cf. also ibid., col. 1607.
78 Ibn Arabi's (1165–1240) approach to the rapport between God and the world (creator and creation) has been analyzed by Salman Bashier in *Ibn al-Arabi's Barzakh. The Concept of the Limit and the Relationship between God and the World*, (Albany: State University of New York Press, 2004). For the relation between the positions of Ibn al-Arabi and Averroës, see Bashier, ibid. p. 52–7. While Ibn Arabi, as a "Muslim mystic," took little interest in philosophers, he was nonetheless profoundly moved by his encounter with Averroës. (see Bashier, ibid., pp. 66–7). Regarding these meetings, and Ibn al-Arabi's understanding of the difference between his position and that of Averroës, see William Chittick, *The Sufi Path of Knowledge*, (Albany: State University of New York Press: 1984) 284. Indeed, his awareness of this difference can only underscore the high regard Ibn Arabi had for Averroës: "Praise belongs to God, that I should have lived in a time which I saw one whose God has given mercy from Him, and taught Him knowledge from Him" (ibid.). (Also see J. Puig, "Materials on Averroes' Circle," *Journal of Near Eastern Studies* 51 [no. 32] 241–60, notably 250, note 68). Moreover, Ibn Arabi was utterly convinced of the close relation between the philosopher, Averroës, and his faith as a believer.

6 Ghazali and Averroës in Muslim society

1 They both distance themselves from the Maliki school, according to which the Qur'an is only comprehensible in the light of the Meccan traditions.
2 Averroës, *Decisive Treatise* § 43; Discours, § 54; Ghazali, *Critère décisif*, § 66.
3 Given the propensity for power, the need to take control, which Ghazali sees ensconced in the human heart (as F. Jabre notes in *La notion de la Marifa chez Ghazali* [Beyrouth: Dar El Machreq, 2è éd., 1986]. Chapter 2), left to themselves, human beings can only be at odds with one another. So even an

incompetent and oppressive sultan is preferable to the real risk of anarchy. So M. Hogga calls attention to the limits of any reform, insisting that "reform is not only impeded by a moralizing perception of things, but compromised as well by political options, which are practically reduced to zero" (op. cit., 173). This criticism puts to one side the fundamental position of Ghazali, for whom the limits of any social reform are already given in human nature, called by God to a free act by which one becomes a servant of God in renouncing oneself. I would call attention to the profound similarity between Ghazali's social vision and that of Augustine, for both are convinced that the key to the public square and to the human heart are identical. "So two loves have made two cities . . ." (Augustine, *City of God*, XIV, 28, PL. 436 b). Similar to Ghazali, Augustine was convinced that the only program by which Christians can guide their lives is one which prepares them for eternal beatitude by following the divine promises. This beatitude will be the lot of Christians after the judgment, since only the vision of God can recognize the merits of each person, given that He is the judge who responds to the hoes of all: "indeed, what other goal could be ours but that of arriving at the kingdom without end?" (*City of God*, XXII, 30, PL 804).

4 Regarding this mission, see *Al-Ghazali's Deliverance from Error* (Louisville, KY: Fons Vitae, 2005) 90 ff.
5 *Decisive Treatise*, §60; *Discours décisif*, § 72.
6 Ibid.
7 Ghazali, *On the Boundaries* § XII, pp. 123–4; *Le critère décisif*, p. 52.
8 Translator's note: since the author worked with M. Hogga, *Le critère décisif de distinction entre l'islam et le manichéisme* (Bordeaux: Bibliothèque universitaire, 1983), which sometimes differs from the English translation of Sherman A. Jackson, *On the Boundaries of Theological Tolerance in Islam*, Studies in IslamicPhilosophy, Nomanul Haq (Karachi: Oxford University Press, 2002), for consistency with the original, I utilize sometimes one translation and sometimes another, noting the pagination for each in parentheses in the text: B = *Boundaries*; C = *Critère*; so here (B85, C11).
9 *On the Boundaries* § I, pp. 86–7: "Yet they said about it: 'It is but tales of the ancients'" (see Qur'an 6:25, 8:31, 16:24, 27:68); *Critère décisif*, p. 12.
10 *Discours décisif*, 179–80, notes 11, 40 and 45; cf. Chapter 4 above.
11 *Decisive Treatise* § 36, 55, 58; *Discours décisif* § 47, 67 and 70, notes 45 (p. 188), 46 and 48 (189).
12 *Decisive Treatise* § 11, *Discours décisi.*, § 16.
13 On the central role played by "polyvalent terms" in Averroës' philosophy, see Olivier Leaman, *Averroës and His Philosophy* (London: Curzon, 1998), Introduction and pp. 179–98.
14 *Decisive Treatise* § 30, *Discours décisif*, § 41, 191–2, note 53.
15 Al-Kashf, 79. Cf. *Discours décisif*, 204, note 103.
16 *Decisive Treatise* § 30, *Discours décisif*, § 41.
17 *Kitab al-Kashf an Manahij Al-Adilla* (*Le livre de l'exposition des méthodes de la preuve*), 124–7. ET in. G. Hourani, *Averroës, On the Harmony . . .*, op. cit., 78–81.
18 *Decisive Treatise* § 14, *Discours décisif*, § 23.
19 *Kitab al-Kashf*, op. cit., 124; ET in Hourani, op. cit., 78.
20 Hourani, ibid., 79.

21 Ibid., 79–80.
22 *Kitab al-Kashf*, op. cit., 125–6.
23 Ibid.,125; ET in Hourani, op. cit., 80.
24 Hourani, op. cit., 80 and note 233; *Kitab al-Kashf*, op. cit., 126, § 1–2.
25 *Kitab al-Kashf*, op. cit., 126 § 6.
26 *Decisive Treatise* § 35, *Discours décisif*, § 45.
27 *Decisive Treatise* § 36, *Discours décisif*, § 46
28 *Decisive Treatise* § 60, *Discours décisif*, § 72
29 R. Arnaldez, *Averroës, A Rationalist in Islam*, op. cit., translated by David Streight, (Notre Dame, IN: University Notre Dame Press, 2000), esp. p. 25.
30 *Decisive Treatise* § 60, *Discours décisif*, § 72.
31 *Decisive Treatise* § 52, *Discours décisif*, § 64.
32 *Decisive Treatise* § 53, *Discours décisif*, § 65.
33 *Decisive Treatise* § 54, *Discours décisif*, § 66.
34 *Decisive Treatise* § 49, *Discours décisif*, § 61.
35 For this approach, see the Introduction of Alain de Libera to *Le Livre du discours décisif*, Flammarion, Paris, 1996. "This text is clearly addressed to the powers . . . to help expedite and to celebrate politico-religious reform" (p.12 with note 18).
36 Judges who "force themselves" recapitulates the title of Averroës' book: "A beginning for those who 'force themselves' and an end for those who attain it" (*Bidaya Al-Mujtahid wa-nihaya Al-Muqtasid*), (Cairo: Maktabat al-kulliyat al-Azhariyya, 1394 H/1974).
37 Cf. R. Arnaldez, op. cit., p. 21; M. Fakhry, *Averroës, Ibn Rushd, His Life, Works and Influence*. (Oxford: One World, 2001), Introduction pp. xii, xvi, then 1–2, 114, 116, 124; D. Urvoy, *Ibn Rushd (Averroès)*, trans. O. Stewart, op. cit., 2, 12, 13, 17, 65, 66, 67, 69.
38 *Decisive Treatise* § 60, *Discours décisif*, § 72.
39 *Decisive Treatise* § 54, *Discours décisif*, § 66.
40 On Ibn Tûmart and Almohad ideology, see Averroës, *Discours décisif*, annexe, pp. 87–96; D. Urvoy, *Penseurs d'al-Andalus. La vie intellectuelle à Cordoue et Séville aux temps des empires berbères (fin XIè–début XIIIè siècles)* (Toulouse: CNRS/PUM, 1990).
41 Averroës, *Al-Kashf*, op. cit., 79; cf. *Discours décisif*, 204, note 103.
42 I would share the view of L. Gauthier in *La théorie d'Ibn Ruschd (Averroès) sur les rapports de la religion et de la philosophie*, (Paris: Leroux, 1909; Vrin, 1983) 90–1. The author insists that the homage Averroës pays to the Almohad polity can only be understood in a context wherein the Andalusian leaders had long lost faith in the founding principles of the Islamic movement. Yet I would also suggest that they could have had a simplistic view of the utopian strain of the founder
43 Averroës, in Roger Arnaldez *A Rationalist in Islam*, op. cit., p. 3.
44 Cf. M. Fakhry, op. cit., p. 116.

Bibliography

Primary sources

Abu Hamid ibn Muhammad al-Ghazali

Tahafut al-Falasifa (*L'incohérence des philosophes*). Beyrouth: Bouyges, 1927; Le Caire: Dunya, 1947.

The Incoherence of the Philosophers, trans. M. E. Marmura. Provo, UT: Brigham Young University Press, 2000.

Ihya' Ulum ad-Din. Halabi: Le Caire, 1er vol., 1346; 2ème, 3ème et 4ème vol., 1352/1933. French partial translation: *La revivification des sciences de la religion.* Analysis and index by G.-H. Bousquet. Paris: Librairie Max Besson, 1955.

—— English translation of Book 35: *Faith in Divine Unity and Trust in Divine Providence,* translated with an introduction and notes by D. B. Burrell, C.S.C. Louisville, KY: Fons Vitae, 2001.

—— French translation: *Livre de la crainte et de l'espérance,* éd. Halabi, Livre 33, tome IV. English translation: *Ghazali's Book of Fear and Hope,* tr. William McKane. Leyden: Brill, 1962.

Al-Maqsad al-Asna fi Asma Allah Al-Husna. Le Caire, 1324.

—— English translation: *Al-Ghazali on the Ninety-nine Beautiful Names of God* translated with notes by D. B. Burrell and N. Daher. Cambridge: Islamic Texts Society, 1995/Louisville, KY: Fons Vitae, 2000.

Al-Qistas al-Mustaqim (*La balance juste*). Le Caire, 1900; Beyrouth: Victor Chelhot, 1959.

—— French translation by Victor Chelhot, in *Bulletin d'Études orientales* (15) 7–98.

Faysal al-Tafriqa Bayn al-Islam wa az-Zandaqa (*Le décret de la distinction entre l'islam et les hypocrites*). Le Caire: Jamahir al-Ghawali, 1934.

—— English translation: *On the Boundaries of Theological Tolerance in Islam,* Sherman A. Jackson, [coll. *Studies in Islamic Philosophy,* S. Nomanul Haq]. Karachi: Oxford University Press, 2002.

—— French translation: *Le critère décisif de distinction entre l'islam et le manichéisme*. Présentation, traduction, étude sémiotique par Mustapha Hogga. Bordeaux: Bibliothèque universitaire, 1983.

Al-Munqidh min Al-Dalal (Erreur et délivrance). Le Caire: Qasim, 1952; Beyrouth: UNESCO, 1959.

—— English translations: W. M. Watt, *The Faith and Practice of Al-Ghazali*. London: G. Allen and Unwin, 1967; R. J. McCarthy, *Freedom and Fulfillment*, Boston: Twayne Publishers, 1980, re-issued as *Al-Ghazali's Deliverance from Error*. Louisville, KY: Fons Vitae, 2005.

—— French translation: Farid Jabre, *Erreur et délivrance*, with introduction and notes (2ème éd) Beyrouth: Commission libanaise pour la traduction des chefs-d'œuvre, 1969.

Abu'l Walid Muhammad ibn Ahmed ibn Rushd, or Averroës

Averroës, L'intelligence et la pensée, sur le De anima, presentation and translation by Alain de Libera. Paris: Garnier-Flammarion, 1998.

Aristotle: works listed by title with Bekker pagination accessible to all standard editions.

Bidaya Al-Mujtahid wa Nihayat Al-Munqtasid (Le commencement pour celui qui s'efforce et la fin pour celui qui se satisfait). (3ème éd) Le Caire: Halabi, 1960.

Damima al-Ilm al-Ilahiy (Appendice à la science de la métaphysique), ed. G. F. Hourani. Leyden: E. J. Brill, 1959.

—— English translation in G. F. Hourani, *Averroës on the Harmony of Religion and Philosophy*. London: Luzac & Co., 1976.

G. F. Hourani (éd.), *Fasl al-Maqal wa Taqrir Ma bayn al-Shariah wa l-Hikma min al-Ittisal (Le discours décisif du rapport entre religion et philosophie)*. Leyden: E. J. Brill, 1959.

—— English translation by G. F. Hourani under the title: *Averroës on the Harmony of Religion and Philosophy*. London: Luzac & Co., 1976.

—— English translation: *The Book of the Decisive Treatise Determining the Connection Between the Law and Wisdom with Epistle Dedicatory*, tr. Charles Butterworth [English/Arabic]. Provo, UT: Brigham Young University Press, 2001.

—— French translation under the title *Le Livre du discours décisif*, introduction par Alain de Libera, trad. inédite, notes et dossier par Marc Geoffroy. Paris: Flammarion, 1996.

Al-Kashf an manahij Al-Adillah (Exposition des méthodes de la preuve), Al-Matbaat al-Rahmaniyyah. Le Caire, n.d.

Al-Kashf an marahiij Al-Adilla (Le livre de l'exposition des méthodes de la preuve). Beyrouth: Dar el-Afaq ad-Jahida, 1402 h/1982.

—— partial English translation by G. F. Hourani. London: Luzac & Co., 1961.

Ibn Rushd's Metaphysics, a translation with introduction of *Ibn Rushd's*

Commentary on Aristotle's Metaphysics, Book Lamda (XII), by Charles Genequand. Leyden: F. J. Brill, 1984.

Averroës' De Substantia Orbis, Critical edition of the Hebrew text with English translation and commentary by Arthur Hyman. Cambridge, MA and Jerusalem, 1986.

Averroës on Plato's Republic, translated with an introduction and notes by R. Lerner. Ithaca and London: Cornell University Press, 1974.

Tahafut at-Tahafut (Incohérence de l'incohérence), Bibliotheca Arabica Scholasticorum, Arabic Series no. 3, ed. M. Bouyges. Beyrouth: Imprimerie catholique, 1930.

—— English translation by Van den Bergh: *Averroës' Tahafut al-Tahafut (The Incoherence of the Incoherence)*. London: Luzac, 1954.

Secondary sources

Allard, M. "Le rationalisme d'Averroès d'après une étude sur la Création," *Bulletin d'études orientales*, no. 14, 1952–54. Institut français de Damas: Damas, 1954.

——. *Le problème des attributs divins dans la doctrine d'Achari*. Beyrouth: Imprimerie catholique, 1965.

Arkoun, Mohamed. "Révélation, vérité et histoire d'après l'œuvre de Ghazali," in *Essais sur la pensée islamique*. Paris: Maisonneuve & Larose, 1973.

Arnaldez, Roger. *A Rationalist in Islam*, tr. D. Streight. Notre Dame, IN: University of Notre Dame Press, 2000.

Bashier, Salman. Ibn al-Arabi's Barzakh. *The Concept of the Limit and the Relationship between God and the World*. Albany, NY: State University of New York Press, 2004.

Bauloye (Lüttich), L. "Note sur la doctrine ruschdienne de la substance, d'après le Grand Commentaire de la Métaphysique," *Averroës (1126–1198) oder der Triumph der rationalismus*, [Internationales Symposium, Heidelberg, 1998] ed. Raif Georges Khoury. Heidelberg, 2002.

Bello, A. *The Medieval Islamic Controversy between Philosophy and Orthodoxy*. Leyden: E. J. Brill, 1989.

Burrell, David. "Avicenna," in *Companion to Philosophy in the Middle Ages*, ed. by J. J. E. Gracia and T. B. Loone. Oxford: Blackwell, 2003.

Campanini, Massimo. "Al-Ghazali" in *Introduction to Islamic Philosophy*, tr. Caroline Higgitt. Edinburgh: Edinburgh University Press, 2008.

Chittick, William. *The Sufi Path of Knowledge*. Albany, NY: State University of New York Press, 1984.

Cooper, J.-M. "Hypothetical Necessity and Natural Teleology," in *Philosophical Issues in Aristotle's Biology*, ed. by A. Gotthalf and J.-G. Lennox. Cambridge: Cambridge University Press, 1987.

Cruz Hernandez, M. "La crítica de Averroes al despotismo oligárquico andaluz," in *Al Encuentro de Averroes*, ed. A. M. Lorca. Madrid: Editorial Trotta, 1993.

Dabashi, H. "Ayn al-Qudât Hamadanni and The Intellectual Climate at his Times," in *History of Islamic Philosophy*, ed. by S. H. Nasr and O. Leaman. London: Routledge, 1996.

Dartary, Farhad. *The Isma'ilis: Their History and Doctrine.* Cambridge: Cambridge University Press, 1990.

Gauthier, L. *La théorie d'Ibn Ruschd (Averroès) sur les rapports de la religion et de la philosophie.* Paris: Leroux, 1909; Vrin, 1983.

Fakhry, M. (2001) *Averroes, Ibn Rushd, His Life, Works and Influence.* Oxford: One World.

Frank, R. *Al-Ghazali and the Asharite School.* Durham, NC: Duke University Press, 1994.

Geoffroy, M. "L'almohadisme théologique d'Averroès," *Archives d'histoire doctrinale et littéraire du Moyen Age* (66) 1999.

Gill, M.-L. *Aristotle on Substance, the Paradox of Unity.* Princeton: Princeton University Press, 1989.

Goldziher, I. *Vorlesung über den Islam.* Heidelberg, 1910.

Goldziher, I. Introduction à D. Luciani (éd.), *Le livre de Mohammed ibn Tûmart, Mahdi des Almohade.* Alger, 1903.

Gotthalf, A. "Aristotle's Conception of Final Causality," in *Philosophical Issues in Aristotle's Biology,* ed. A. Gotthalf and J.-G. Lennox. Cambridge: Cambridge University Press, 1987.

Graham, D-W. *Aristotle's Two Systems.* Oxford: Clarendon Press, 1987.

Gutas, D. *Greek Thought Arabic Culture, The Graeco-Arabic Translation Movement in Baghdad and Early Abbasid Society.* London: Routledge, 1998.

Hogga, M. "Orthodoxie, subversion et réforme en Islam," *Etudes musulmanes* (34) 1933.

Ibn, Tufayl. *Hayy ibn Yaqzan [A Philosophical Tale],* trans. Lenn Goodman. Los Angeles: Gee Tee Bee, 1976.

Inati, Shams. "Logic," in *History of Islamic Philosophy*, eds. Sayyed Hossein Nasr and Oliver Leaman. London: Routledge, 1996, 802–23.

Jabre, F. *La notion de la Maarifa chez Ghazali,* 2è éd. Beyrouth: Dar El Machreq,1986.

——. *La vie et l'œuvre de Ghazali reconsidérées à la lumière des Tabaqât de Subki.* Cairo: Institut dominicain d'études orientales [IDEO], 1954.

Jolivet, J. "Divergences entre les métaphysiques d'Ibn Rushd et d'Aristote," *Arabica* (29) 1982, 225–45.

Khatami, Sayyed Mohammed. *La religion et la pensée prises au piège de l'autocratie.* Louvain-Paris: Peeters, 2005.

Kogan, B. S. *Averroës and the Metaphysics of Causation.* Albany, NY: State University of New-York Press, 1985.

Lazarus-Yafeh, H. *Studies in al-Ghazali.* Jerusalem: Magnes Press of Hebrew University, 1973.

Leaman, Oliver. *Averroës and His Philosophy.* London: Curzon, 1998.

Lennox, J.-G. "Teleology, Chance and Aristotle's Theory of Spontaneous Generation," *Journal of the History of Philosophy*, 20.

Makdisi, G. *Hanabalite Islam, Studies on Islam*, tr. and ed. M. Swarz. Oxford: Oxford University Press, 1981.

Muhajirani, Abbas. "Twelve Shi'ite Imams," in *History of Islamic Philosophy*, eds. Sayyed Hossein Nasr and Oliver Leaman. London: Routledge, 1996, 119–43.

Pinès, S. "Philosophy," in *The Cambridge History of Islam*, eds. P. M. Holt *et al*. Cambridge: Cambridge University Press: 1970. vol. 2, 814.

Puig, J. "Materials on Averroës's circle," *Journal of Near Eastern Studies* 51, 1992, 241–60.

Siauve, M. L. *L'amour de Dieu chez Ghazali*. Paris: Vrin, 1986.

Stroumsa, Sarah. "Philosophes almohades? Averroès, Maïmonide et l'idéologie almohade," *Los Almohade: Problemas y perspectivas*, vol. II, Patrice Cressier Maribel Fierro y Louis Molina (éds), *Estudios arabes e islamicos, monografias, 2005.

Touati, Charles. *Multiple Averroès*. Paris, 1978.

Urvoy, D. "La pensée d'Ibn Tûmart," *Bulletin d'Études orientales*, Damas (37) 1974.

——. *Le monde des oulémas andalous du V/XIème au VII/XIIIème siècles*. Genève, 1978.

——. *Penseurs d'al-Andalus. La vie intellectuelle à Cordoue et Séville aux temps des empires berbères (fin XIè–début XIIIè siècles)* Toulouse: CNRS/PUM, 1990.

——. *Ibn Rushd*, tr. O. Stewart. London: Routledge, 1991.

——. *Averroès, les ambitions d'un intellectuel musulman*. Paris: Flammarion, 1998.

Watt, W. M. "al-Ghazali," *Encyclopedia of Islam Vol. II.*, 1040.

Whittingham, M. "Al-Ghazali on Jews and Christians," in *The Three Rings*, eds. B. Roggema, M. Poorthuis and P. Valkenberg. Leuven: Peeters, 2005.

Index